THE BALL PLAYER

Bill Whittington

Order this book online at www.trafford.com
or email orders@trafford.com

Most Trafford titles are also available at major online book retailers.

Print information available on the last page.

ISBN: 978-1-6987-1276-5 (sc)
ISBN: 978-1-6987-1275-8 (hc)
ISBN: 978-1-6987-1274-1 (e)

Library of Congress Control Number: 2022916051

Trafford rev. 08/26/2022

www.trafford.com
North America & international
toll-free: 844-688-6899 (USA & Canada)
fax: 812 355 4082

Contents

Special Thanks

I would like to extend an acknowledgment and special thanks to those individuals who helped make this book a reality: Billy Ford, Tom Nunley, Frank Capra, Vernon Harold Ford, Harold Furr, James Howard Hooks Jr., Richard Lapish, Richard Lefler, Bryant Parnell Jr., Jerry Pierce, Rodney Quesenberry, Willard Mauney Sr., Luke Mauney, Richard Mauney, Marvin Mauney, Harold Mauney, Rick McClamrock, Hank Utley, Eva Whittington-Self, James Manuel Whittington Sr., Mae Belle Whittington, Ted Whittington, and Gene Kermit Verble Sr.

If I have omitted anyone that added credit to this book, I humbly apologize. Unfortunately, most of those mentioned in this section are no longer with us.

If you would like to know more about these people, I have included a section at the end called About the People.

Introduction

When my homesickness could no longer be diminished, I knew it was time to take another journey home. The moment I left work and rolled out on the road, hundreds of fond memories and independent thoughts started to take effect. I felt like a wild animal that had been released from captivity. My thoughts of home and of my boyhood seemed like ancient history. It was only then I realized it had been fifteen years since I had been home.

As the trip progressed, I started visualizing the old neighborhood and that five-room house on Linden Avenue where I grew up. After spending eighteen years there and graduating from high school in 1972, I joined the military and served for twenty-seven years.

During those years of service, I traveled all over the United States and spent time in several foreign countries. The world that I had left behind seemed smaller than a postage stamp, yet you would be surprised how many memories I rediscovered within that small postage stamp.

I had visited home many times before while in service, and like those previous visits, a plethora of thoughts and memories would spring forth. However, when I left work that February evening, there were so many memories that began to unfold, it was almost impossible to keep up with the influx of those separate slices of life that I could recall.

I planned to reassemble those detached pieces of that large jigsaw puzzle and put them in their proper place. I wanted to find my old self and see how many things were the way they used to be.

When familiar landmarks came into view along the way, they miraculously unlocked memory patterns that had been previously closed. Those thoughts and associated emotions returned as vividly as if I had experienced them only the day before. Yet had I not seen that familiar building, crossed over that old bridge, or gazed down into the river, there is no telling how long those memories would have remained suppressed.

The closer I got to home, the farther back in time those memories took me because I had been gone so long, it was difficult to determine which memories were real or just imagined, and I began to question if some of those events actually happened.

Unfortunately, I heard they had torn down the Red Pig restaurant, but the most disturbing news was they had demolished our old elementary school since I had been away. I thought, *who did they think they were? Who gave them permission to tear down Hartsell School? I never would have given them permission to do such a thing.*

Many of my classmates had the opportunity to gather bricks or bits and pieces of memorabilia while the school was being torn down. However, I knew it would be difficult for me to see an empty piece of land where my school used to stand. My classmates had time to adapt to the change, whereas I had not.

The sun was beginning to rise when I crossed the Carolina line, and excitement was building like the crescendo of a large orchestra. I was in overdrive, and there wouldn't have been any way I could have slept, regardless how tired I was. There were so many things that I had to see and do in such a short time. I planned to visit my old neighborhood, drive over to see Howard Hooks, but sadly, I wanted to pay my respects to a childhood friend, Billy Edwards, who was resting in the Oakwood Cemetery.

On the way to Howard's, I drove past my old house on Linden Avenue. I stopped my truck but didn't get out. It was at this moment I remembered a powerful dream I had during my military days, while I was stationed overseas. It was a futuristic-type dream, and in that dream, I happened to be looking at my house from across the street, just like I was now from inside the truck.

In the dream, my home was abandoned, and I could see cobwebs draped across the dusty furniture through the windows.

For some reason, I could not go inside because I realized that my parents had passed away. The same was true when I was staring at the house during this trip, even though there weren't any cobwebs, but like in that dream, I could not go inside because someone else was living in our old home. That dream had just become a living reality; it struck a chord deep in my soul, and it was painful for me to stay there any longer.

This trip meant a lot; I didn't want to miss anything, knowing that this would probably be the last time I would visit my birthplace. I drove through historic Concord and proceeded toward Richfield along Highway 49, where Howard currently resided. While driving north on Highway 49, the Mount Pleasant High School seemed to appear out of nowhere, as if I had totally forgotten that it was ever there. This site could not be passed up; so I pulled over, got out of the truck, and walked out onto the baseball field.

Baseball was a very large piece of that childhood puzzle, and after I walked out on that field, I knew I was finally at home, as if I had never left. Memories started flowing in at high speed; Mount Pleasant was one of our high school opponent teams within the Rocky River Conference.

Once again, I was whisked to another time. I remembered that wonderful sound a bat makes when a baseball was hit well, followed by a loud pop when the ball was caught deep in the pocket of the glove or a mitt. I could almost hear chatter emanating from each bench, the spectators' shouts, whistles, and catcalls coming from the fans in the bleachers along the bank while the crowd rooted for their favorites.

As I stood on the mound, I turned and imagined I saw the dust fly up after Don L. Means slid into second. While standing in the batter's box, I pictured Jim Ritchie, the Mount Pleasant pitcher, toeing the rubber on the mound while taking his signal from the catcher.

I cannot recall how long I was out there, but those memories eventually waned, which left me stranded on that Mount Pleasant Baseball Field all alone. Those memories were wonderful; I regret they faded. Had those ballplayers stayed around a little longer, we might have been able to finish the game. Then I realized that this particular game had already been played, and the score had been decided thirty-eight years earlier.

Over time, I had lost track with my teammates and had no idea where they were now or how many were still alive. While standing on that deserted baseball field, I experienced sad feelings, similar to those felt by an old actor while standing on an empty stage where he used to perform, or what a sailor might experience while revisiting his old ship, or how an old soldier might feel standing on an abandoned battlefield where he once fought. After those memories passed, I knew it was time to continue my journey on down the road.

When I pulled into Howard's driveway, I saw my old friend standing on the front porch and noticed the physical changes that age offered. I am sure he noticed changes in my appearance as well, but it was the same old Howard, and it was good to see him.

After he invited me in, we talked for a while and covered many of the changes that had taken place since I had been away. We reminisced and talked about old friends, especially the ones who weren't with us anymore. Then he walked over to his bookshelf and pulled down three thick photo albums that contained many of our fathers' team pictures when they played in the Carolina Textile Baseball League.

Some photos were labeled with dates that included rosters of names; however, most pictures were not labeled nor dated, so we had to guess who some of the ballplayers were and estimate when the pictures were taken. We were amazed that we could still name many of the grand old players, but at an earlier time, we would have been able to name everyone in those pictures.

The pictures were black and white, so we could only imagine the color schemes of the uniforms. We were unsure where most photographs were taken because many were taken on ball fields that had long since vanished by the time Howard and I came along, and only a select few of those ballplayers were still alive.

There were nostalgic team pictures of Roberta, Mount Pleasant, the 1947 Morganton Aggies, and the 1951 Salisbury Bomber All Stars. My favorite was called the Big Three, which featured Shad

Whittington, Harold Furr, and Vernon Ford, the second, third, and fourth hitters of the Roberta lineup.

To some, it was only a photo gallery of an obscure group of ballplayers that had seen their day. But to me, it meant much more. I knew these people; when I was growing up, I saw them almost every day. This represented true-to-life North Carolina history, my heritage displayed in pictorial forms. Those pictures captured a time when baseball was rough and raw because the people in the pictures were rough and raw. I realized that I finally found what I had been searching for all along.

I wondered if it was too late, that maybe their memories were lost to time or forgotten forever. Suddenly, I thought what if someone could tell their stories the way I heard them told and recapture some of that Carolina history? After leafing through more pictures, I decided to do just that, and my mind drifted back to the time and place where this story began.

Chapter 1

Franklin Mill Hill's New Arrival

Eva Whittington happened to notice an old elm tree, just on the other side of Robinson Street, while gazing out through her mill house window. As her labor pains eased somewhat, she noticed the leaves of that tree were still dark green despite the long hot summer. Normally, by September, those leaves would have started to change colors, but the elm appeared to be tired and bowed, much the same way that she felt.

As she continued to gaze, her mind wandered back to an earlier time. She thought about Titus Hunneycutt, the first man she had cared for, when she lived way down in Stanly County. It was through their union she had given birth to her firstborn son, Clifford, in December 1895, when she was about seventeen years old.

That relationship soured, and later she met and married a man who was twenty-two years older, named William Monroe Whittington, born in Anson County on May 13, 1856. The folks on the mill hill didn't call him William, they just called him Bud. Eva had given Bud two proud sons: Clarence Lee, in 1903, and Willie, in 1911.

Bud and Eva were among the many who migrated from agricultural fields in other counties and gravitated toward the industrialized cotton mills. When Will was born, the family worked at the Roberta Cotton Mill, but not long afterward, they took jobs at the Franklin Mill and were assigned a mill house on Robinson Street.

Eva was around thirty-seven years old when she was expecting her fourth child that could come at any time. She slowly turned her gaze from the window and looked down at her rough and calloused hands. She never complained about hard work. What good would it have done? If she could live her life over again, she probably would not have changed a thing because this was the only life she ever knew. Her options were limited. Life had not been kind to this rugged but petite woman; she absorbed all the abuse a dominating husband and an unforgiving society offered as if it were her lot in life.

She stood five-feet-two, her eyes were dark, she had long black hair. She appeared to be more Indian than Caucasian, although it was reported that she was half Cherokee. Most North Carolinians knew there were many from this proud and noble tribe who didn't take part in the journey of the Trail of Tears during Andrew Jackson's forced march westward. Many of Eva's Indian forefathers remained in the Carolina hills, married locals, or formed their own indigenous communities.

As Eva grew closer to her delivery, Nancy Best was summoned to aid with the task of bringing this newborn into the world. Nancy was hired as a servant who resided with the Whittingtons, along with Joel Doster, another boarder. Nancy would fulfill the duties of midwife on this special day.

Home deliveries were quite common up to and a little after World War 2. Hardly anybody went to the hospital in Downtown Concord because many of the locals believed that visiting that hospital was the kiss of death. Doctors would make home visits and aide in deliveries or visit with the patients as soon as they could to complete the necessary paperwork for the birth certificate. The date of birth was usually recorded in the family Bible. The fee for normal deliveries was about a dollar-quite a bit of money in 1914.

With Nancy's help, Eva's child was born. He was a healthy boy, and after Nancy put this baby in his mother's arms, tears of pride streamed down Eva's face. Her husband was away working in the spinning department, on the first shift, in the Franklin Mill. To him, having babies was the woman's job; however, he would see his son as soon as the shift was over.

Earlier that day, Eva told her sons, Clarence and Willie, to stay close by because a surprise might be coming later in the day. Nancy cleaned then wrapped the newborn in a crouched blanket just before the doctor drove up in a horse-drawn buggy and came in to visit his patient.

Old doc was happy to see that everything was all right. Just then, Clarence and Willie came into the room, and Eva Hunneycutt Whittington held her newborn up and said, ***"Boys, I won't you to meet your new brother, James Manual Whittington."***

This event took place on September 27, 1914. This was how my father arrived on the Franklin Mill Hill, and as he grew, so did the country.

Chapter 2

Signs of the Times

Cotton mills were very plentiful around Concord. In the early 1900s, mills were scattered throughout the state but were very prominent in the Piedmont region of North Carolina, a prime example of the Industrial Revolution trying to find its place in an agrarian society. The housing projects around most cotton mills were villages or self-contained communities, similar to base housing found on military installations today. If one worked for the mill long enough, that person and that person's family could rent a mill house, and a portion of money would be withheld from the employee's check to pay the rent.

The Franklin Mill was originally called the Coleman Manufacturing Company, owned by Warren Clay Coleman, an African American entrepreneur. The mill was purchased by James W. Cannon in 1904.

Franklin, known as D. F. Cannon, gave James his start in business, and James Cannon named the mill Franklin for his elder brother's namesake. After James Cannon passed away, his son Charles Albert Cannon became the president of Cannon Mills. Charlie Cannon bought out many mills in surrounding counties, including mills as far away as South Carolina and Georgia, and forged the Cannon Textile Empire.

If a mill was owned by Cannon, that mill was later given a plant number, such as the Franklin Mill, Plant 9; the Gibson Mill, Plant 6; the Cabarrus Mill, Plant 5; or Plant 1 in Kannapolis. Even after Cannon bought other mills, the older people referred to those mills by original names.

These textile mills were located beside railroad tracks so they could receive the raw cotton, and the finished products could be downloaded onto boxcars along the tracks. At an earlier time, those products were transported to and from the Odell-Locke Mill through the streets of Concord by mule-drawn wagons.

The housing projects were commonly called mill hills, even if they weren't located on a hill. The workers lived in a two or three-room house made of wood, with a wood-or a coal-burning heater located in the living room. Franklin community homes were fully electrified, while other houses in the state still used oil lamps. If a power outage occurred, the generators that ran the mill could also power the housing area.

Some select mill houses, where the overseers lived in the Franklin community, had indoor toilets. The majority of the mill houses did not have indoor plumbing; they had outhouses in the backyard. Those residents drew water from local wells or nearby springs, washed their clothes in a huge pot of heated water outside in the yard, scrubbed their clothes on a washboard, and hung the clothes on a line to dry.

When those outhouses filled, a honey wagon came along and would suck out the waste product, which was sprayed over local fields or dumped into the branch that flowed along Robinson Street. Many mills dumped their sewage into adjacent creeks. The branch that flowed past the Franklin Mill emptied farther downstream into the Dutch Buffalo Creek, and because of this, Buffalo Creek smelled so bad, the people in and around Concord nicknamed it the Shit Creek.

Toilet paper was an item not so readily available or was seldom used, so old newspapers or Sears and Roebuck catalogs were used instead. People would jokingly say, "It took two red corncobs to wipe with, and a white corn cob was used to see if the job was finished properly."

This was more a reality than a joke.

The houses were located close to the mill so people could walk to and from work. During the late teens and early '20s, car sheds or garages were not built because most workers could not afford a car. Garages were added later. The people worked the mills and the fields to supplement their existence, and it was not uncommon for a family to finish work in the mill and then have to plow or seed the fields after they came home. The mills didn't pay much, but it was consistent work, and the checks came in on time.

If a person who is familiar with Concord or Cabarrus County region today were miraculously transported back in time, to 1914, that person would have had trouble navigating around those parts. The landscape would have been devoid of many roads and landmarks that our contemporaries would be accustomed to. Most of the urban development found today would have been unclaimed land covered with Southern pines or deciduous trees. Concord would have appeared to be scarcely populated at the time. Cotton and cornfields would have filled the open areas because agricultural products were much more plentiful.

The traveler would notice many roads or thoroughfares would not have existed, and major roads that are present today would have only been a narrow dirt road at the time, so narrow that opposing traffic, the few A- or T-Model Fords and mule-drawn wagons, would have to yield for oncoming traffic. Some roads would have only amounted to a path cut through the woods by wagon wheel ruts. Most bridges had only one lane available, and opposing traffic would have to wait until the other traveler was completely across the bridge before they could proceed.

People walked, rode mules, or were carried by a horse-drawn buggy. A mule would have been cherished much more than a motor vehicle because the mule was easier to maintain and would not be restricted to the roads. It would have taken the traveler much longer to make trips that we take for granted today.

The time traveler would also notice that the language used would have been quite different from what we are accustomed to now. Many things we take for granted today had not been invented or mass-produced during those times. Imagine not having a radio, a television, or a telephone. There might have been a few phones scattered around at some general stores but very few. Buses were out of the question, and trains would have provided long cross-county transportation.

Radios became more prominent later, in the '30s, and only a select few residents took the local newspaper. Many mill hands could neither read nor write, so they might ask a neighbor who subscribed to the paper as to what was going on in the world. Could you imagine seeing a congregation of people gathered around a mill worker's porch while that neighbor read them the news aloud? Those present would have passed what they heard throughout the mill hill by word of mouth. Maybe this explains why these people were such great storytellers.

The language they spoke would have been closely tied to their profession, directly linked to an aggregate society and to the region. They spoke farm and mill jargon that most people today might not be able to understand, almost a separate language. Some terms used would have been foreign to users today, words such as *gee* and h*a*, p*ussel gut*, b*ull* and *clay taller*, *cooters*, t*arpons*, *scuppadines*, and *half a bushel*.

Gee and h*a* are verbal commands given to a mule, while the mule had blinders on and be harnessed for plowing. The voice command *gee* would be the signal to turn the mule to the right, and h*a* were the signals for a left turn, which would have been assisted with a rein tug in that direction.

Pussel gut or p*ussel-gutted* would describe a work horse or mule having a large midsection, that appeared to be overfed, but the animal was in dire need of being wormed. *Clay taller* described the land that was difficult to plow because of the content of gray or red clay, and b*ull taller* was slang term for dark clay.

A c*ooter* would be what the locals called a large snapping turtle, and a t*arpon* would be the smaller version or the tortoise. Plenty of people in Cabarrus County still call large snapping turtles cooters to this day. *Scuppadines* were the name of white grapes that grew around the area, and the dark wild grapes were called m*uscadines*. Both types were useful in making wines. And *half a bushel* would be the size of a wooden or metal bucket that could hold a half a bushel of whatever you wanted to carry.

Chapter 3

A Few Early Stories

In 1917, one of my father's buddies, Willard Woodrow Mauney, was born. So it was no mystery as to how Willard got his middle name. Woodrow Wilson was the president of the United States at the time. Before Father reached his third birthday, America jumped into the European War with both feet. The Great War was supposed to be "the war to end all wars," One of Father's earliest memories might have been the sight of the "doughboys," dressed in their uniforms complete with campaign hats and leggings, preparing to leave for World War 1. He definitely would have been old enough to remember their victorious return. They probably appeared to my father as legendary giants, and their stories would be told on the mill hill for years to come.

From June 1918 to December 1920, a deadly flu pandemic swept the globe, killing an estimated 100 million people, about 3 percent of the world's population. My father and his immediate family were untouched by this menace; however, there were many funerals that were attended in Cabarrus and the surrounding counties as a result of this Spanish flu pandemic.

When Grandma worked a field, she took Pappy with her and sat him on a stump near a side row of the garden while she picked corn and butterbeans. He really enjoyed going down to the spring to draw water because Grandma would splash the cool spring water on him, and he would close his eyes, take a deep breath, and start to giggle. Nancy, the hired servant, carried him to the store and treated him with candy.

In 1920, Richard Mauney, Willard's younger brother, was born on Main Street, and Pappy's eldest brother, Clarence Lee, moved out of the Whittington mill house to venture out on his own.

I always called my father Pap, short for Pappy. When Pap told a story, he could imitate all the animals and the sound effects as well. He was a master storyteller and had hundreds of stories to offer. One story took place on the Franklin Mill Hill when Pappy was around five years old. Pap's other elder brother, Will, had gotten bit by a neighbor's dog. His leg was bleeding, and the bite marks were plainly visible. Uncle Will hobbled and cried all the way home to tell his father Bud Whittington.

Bud Whittington stood six feet eleven inches tall and, according to Pappy, was meaner than hell. Pappy didn't have much to say about Grandpa, maybe because he was such a rough customer. Grandpa didn't take any lip from anybody or anything on earth. After he saw Will's leg and listened to his son's explanation, he had only one question: "Where is that dog you talkin' about?"

Grandfather reached up and grabbed the ten-gauge side-by-side double-barreled shotgun called Long Tom, which was hanging over the bedroom door before he left the house. Pappy tagged along just to witness the events that were about to unfold.

After walking down Robinson Street, the trio stopped when my uncle pointed to a dog sitting on the wooden front porch of one of the mill houses. Grandfather asked Willie, "Is that him?"

Uncle Will nodded yes. Grandpa pulled back the hammer of the right-hand barrel of the ten-gauge, and on the other side of that hammer and breach was a shotgun shell filled with number 4 shot. He raised the gun and fired. The shotgun blast slid the dog across the porch, underneath the front porch swing and out into the yard. Just then the mill worker who resided in the home came to the screened door but did not step out onto the porch and yelled, "What in the hell is goin' on out there?"

Grandfather said, "That dog of yours bit my boy, and I shot him. If you have a problem with that, step out on the porch, and I'll do the same for you."

The man thought a little and in a quivering voice, answered, "No, I didn't like that dog much anyhow, he just weren't no count. You did the right thing, Mr. Whittington, you won't hear no more about it from me."

Then Pappy, Uncle Will, and Grandpa turned and walked back up the hill along Robinson Street without saying another word.

Chapter 4

The Mill Hill Boys

Many of Pappy's contemporaries were born and raised on the Franklin Mill Hill: The Mauneys-Luke, Willard, Richard, Marvin Jay, Frank, and Harold-lived on Main Street. The Fords-Shoddy Mac, Clifford, Vernon, Bill, and Thurman-resided on Robinson Street, as well as Bill and Howard Hooks. Conway Foster and Johnson Strube also grew up on Robinson Street. The Leflers-Hulan, James, Link, Charles, and Ralph-lived on Short Street. These people became Pap's lifelong friends, and each in their own way became exceptional baseball players.

The mill hillers were dirt poor but very resilient and resourceful. You would be amazed at how they could work a garden. Pappy and many like him were taught from an early age to become one with the land. Those boys became quite handy with all the farming tools, which helped them immensely with their hand-and-eye coordination that was so magnificently put to use later on the baseball field.

They became excellent hunters and fishermen. They hunted to put food on the table, not for sport. During Father's time, people drew their sustenance from the land, whatever the garden or the woods could provide. They cultivated the land and could grow almost anything. This green thumb was earned through years of trials and errors.

Gardens were planted to have an early summer, a fall, and a winter yield. Winter gardens were full of turnip, mustard, and collard greens, but the creasy greens they collected grew wild. Some of the mill hillers worked as tenant farmers and share-cropped larger farming plots elsewhere.

I would start laughing anytime I heard someone say milkweed because this was a name commonly used when my father explained weakness, was upset with or didn't like a certain person. If any of us failed to eat all our food at the table, Pappy would say, "If you don't eat your food, you will grow up like a milkweed."

He went on to explain that "a milkweed is not as tough as a stalk of corn or even a strand of Johnson grass. Milkweeds snapped the instant you touched them and were good for nothing."

Milkweeds were the most undesirable plant that grew in any garden, a nuisance to farmers and hated with a passion. Calling someone a milkweed was considered a great insult, and the people of Pappy's generation knew exactly what it meant.

Pap said there were many times he was handed a .22 rifle and only three bullets, and Grandpa told him to bring back four squirrels. In other words, every shot had to count. There wasn't a fishing hole or a den tree around that wasn't explored by these youngsters. Those hunters studied and learned the habits of their game. Pap could name almost every tree in the woods and knew which type of tree the squirrels built their nests or made their dens. He knew the hickory nut and scaly-bark trees were where they fed.

Those boys toted their game in oat sacks or just carried their squirrels by holding on to their bushy tails because hunting jackets with game pouches were unheard of. When they came home with a mess of fish or a handful of squirrels, they felt as proud as a caveman that had just slain a woolly mammoth. This meant that the family was going to eat good that night.

Pappy played many games with his buddies on the hill. Their favorite was back-lot baseball, played in some flat between mill houses. They enjoyed playing peggy in the fall and pitched horseshoes year-round. Their horseshoe games were different from the modern version that I learned to play. Pap's teammates had to use discarded mule- or horseshoes, which were much smaller than the store-bought set available in my time. Also, the shoes they used didn't have that prominent hook that enabled the shoe to stay hooked around the metal pin or stake, which they called a stob. The bigger the horse's or mule's feet, the better chance one could toss a ringer.

North Carolina was part of the Bible belt, and its blue laws were strictly enforced. Most businesses closed after twelve o'clock on Wednesdays and remained closed all day Sunday. The Franklin and other mills didn't run on Sundays, nor did the textile leagues play baseball on the Sabbath Day. Any person caught firing a gun on Sunday would be arrested and put in jail for disturbing the peace.

Those Sunday hunters learned to use silent methods, like using a slingshot or by trapping their game in homemade rabbit boxes. When checking rabbit boxes, it was not wise to assume they always had a rabbit in the box. The trapper would open the rabbit box partway, just to see what was inside, because opening a rabbit box containing a full-grown pissed-off coon could mess up someone's day!

The boys made their own slingshots, by locating a choice dogwood tree, with a fork about the right size, and would cut this fork out. This fork was formed by two small limbs growing symmetrically out of each side of the trunk of the tree. The middle piece of wood was cut next, leaving the base and the two limbs extending upward, something in the shape of a large Y. This Y would be called prongs. The upper two limbs of this Y would be wrapped with a wire to get the proper bow.

Many of the other boys would not bake their slingshots, but Pappy would put this piece of wood into an oven and let it bake for several hours at about 350 degrees. When his slingshot came out of the oven, the wood was as hard as a bone and would last forever. After this piece of wood cooled, the upper fork would be cut down to its proper size with a hacksaw because the hardness of the wood would dull or ruin the teeth on a regular saw. Additional cutting would also dull a pocketknife, so the whetstone, leather, and oil would be needed to keep the knife sharp. The finishing touches included cutting a horizontal notch or a slot about an eighth of an inch below the top of the prongs. This cut enabled the shooter to wrap their rubbers horizontally around each prong, or they could wrap the rubbers over the top, and tied off with kite string.

The rubber was taken from an inner tube of an old tire and cut the proper length and width. This red rubber was stronger than the rubber that was available in my time. The final ingredient would be a piece of leather cut from a boot tongue called the bag, with two slits cut near each end so you could thread one end of the rubber through each side of the leather bag and tie the excess off with thread. This bag would be where your small stone or marble would go before you launched or shot the projectile.

Pappy made several slingshots for me, and I learned this special technique. Not many today know how to make a slingshot. I remember the first slingshot that he made and presented to me when I was a boy. It was as if Obi-Wan Kenobi had just handed me a lightsaber. I was very proud. But before I had a chance to rush outside and try out my new weapon, Pap warned, "Now this slingshot is powerful, be careful with it. If you shoot 'somebody in the head with this thing, you could kill 'em, much less put out somebody's eye."

He was right, the slingshot was powerful, and I did not shoot anybody with my slingshot for the longest time. But that is another story.

Now that the boys had slingshots, they could hunt without having to purchase ammunition or make unnecessary noise on Sundays. They learned how to sneak up on the squirrels and would walk slowly along a hedgerow on frosty mornings to find rabbits sitting in their hide sites. The ammunition used varied, from the smoothest small stones that could fly straight and true to marbles, but the best choice of ammunition were steel ball bearings and metal nuts they called taps.

The slingshot could also tame fierce dogs but was the preferred weapon when the boys played war. The boys would form into teams; one team would hide in the woods, and a few moments later, the other team would start their manhunt. When they spotted each other, the slingshot battle would commence. The participants shot green plums or chinaberries, instead of rocks, that would splatter on contact but would still hurt if they were hit. They were such good shots; they never shot one another in the face, so no one ever lost an eye.

The boys knew how to make and use slings, like the one that David used to battle Goliath. Some call this weapon a slingshot, but a sling and a slingshot are two different weapons. A sling was made of two strands of bootlaces or rawhide, and a slingshot uses rubber and wood, and they didn't know how to make rubber in David's time.

A sling was made by taking one end of the leather, rawhide, or bootlace and threading this end through a slit one side of a boot tongue and tying it off. The other end of the rawhide was secured around the middle finger of the throwing hand by use of a slipknot. The other strand of leather or rawhide would have been threaded and tied off to the other side of the boot tongue, but this piece of rawhide had a knot on the end. This knot would be held between the thumb and forefinger of the throwing hand and after the stone was carefully placed in the bag, the user would start a circular motion with their sling. When the proper centrifugal force was achieved, the thrower would release the knotted end of the rawhide, the end held between the thumb and forefinger, and the stone would fly.

This sling was a super extension of one's arm and could propel a rock around 150 miles per hour. One could throw a rock much greater than the distance of a football field, especially with a long sling. The rule is the longer the sling, the greater the power and distance. Unfortunately, the longer-length slings were also very inaccurate and harder to control.

Conversely, the shorter-length slings, about an arm's length, were much more accurate. I believe David used a medium or a short sling when he took out Goliath. The boys became experts with these weapons, but the sling was too dangerous for the boys to use against one another, and because there weren't any large animals to kill, this ancient weapon was used primarily for throwing contests.

Pappy said he could throw a rock through both sides of a wooden outhouse. The rock could easily penetrate one side cleanly and maybe knock an entire board off the outhouse when the stone came out the other side. He went on to add you had to make sure that no one was inside the outhouse, or it's no longer in service, because people didn't appreciate having their outdoor bathrooms torn up.

Those who weren't fortunate enough to have a sling or a slingshot just threw rocks to kill rabbits or squirrels. This might explain why there were so many good baseball pitchers that came off the Franklin Mill Hill. Survival was a strong motivator for success.

Chapter 5

A Meager Formal Education

Getting an education was not such a big deal for many during those early years because the public schools in this area of North Carolina started in earnest around 1911. The Brown-Norcott, Whitehall, and Hartsell schools started as one-room classes that were sponsored by churches or mill communities. Public schools were not available for the generation prior to Pap's era. Some parents didn't see the point in sending their children to school because this would cut in on productivity and hamper the time needed when the crops had to be harvested. Truancy was loosely enforced and didn't become a matter of importance until later in the 1930s.

Sunderland Hall was a private school for young girls, but very few private schools were available for boys. Mill workers could not afford a private school. The closest private school for boys was the Jackson Training School, which provided educational and vocational training for wayward boys convicted of crimes in North Carolina. While achieving their education, they received punishment as adults, so you had to have a bad record to attend.

The closest public schools available to the Franklin Mill were the Hartsell and Brown-Norcott schools. Hartsell School at the time was only a one-room classroom located at the intersection of Sunderland Hall Road and Swink Street.

The Franklin Mill didn't have its own school, so Pap attended the Brown-Norcott School his first year, in 1921, which happened to be the same year James Cannon passed away.

The Brown-Norcott School was located on the other side of Cabarrus Avenue, about where the First Assembly Church is today. This is where Pappy learned to read. I could just hear what his father Bud would say, "Boy, you better mind what that teacher tells you because if you don't, I'm gonna whoop your ass."

The main textbook used would have been *My First Reader.* Harper Lee refers to this book when Jean Louise Finch starts her first day in school. Ned happened to be a prominent character featured in drawings throughout the 1895 McGuffey's *First Reader.* The students saw Ned doing something in the picture, then they were required to read the caption that followed that described the activities, kind of like my generation's version of Dick and Jane.

Pappy and others of his generation, even after they were grown men, referred to Ned many times in an attempt to show someone up or outdo another person. I heard Pappy say many times that guy made him look like Ned in the *First Reader.* In other words, he made him look like a schoolboy.

While watching History Channel one day, I noticed they were interviewing one of the pilots from the Flying Tigers. This pilot said, "Charles Chennault would make most people in aviation look like Ned in the *First Reader.*"

I laughed when I heard that quote, then later I reminisced about it and almost cried. I thought, *What about that?* It had been many years since I had heard quotes about Ned.

Pappy would walk from Robinson to Short Street then follow the Union Cemetery Road until it ended. He had to cut across the old Norcott Baseball Field to get to school. The only other road nearby was Cabarrus Avenue, which ran by the Norcott and Brown mills on the way to Concord. These roads were not paved. The four-lane Highway 29, which currently runs to Charlotte in front of the old county fairgrounds, did not exist at the time and was not constructed until later, during WW2.

Cabarrus Avenue, called State Road 1002 today, would have stopped at the top of the hill. The 601 Bypass, or the Warren Coleman Boulevard, was not even a figment of people's imagination because that road was not cut until 1965. However, where this boulevard intersects State Road 1002 would have marked the original location of the Norcott Mill's first baseball field.

Nancy Best, Father's home nanny, tried to plug educational gaps Father might have had with home studies. In 1922, he returned for his second year at Brown-Norcott school, and in December of the same year, construction for the newly consolidated Hartsell School was taking place at its new location along Swink Street and Hartsell Drive.

This happened to be the same year that Benito Amilcore Andrea Mussolini became Italy's prime minister, an activity not noticed by many at first, but it marked the leading edge of a dark cloud that was starting to form in Europe. The people didn't pay much attention to Mussolini at the time; Pappy didn't notice because he was struggling with his new classroom environment.

For grades 3-6, he attended Hartsell School. When Pap was in the fourth grade, in 1924, two of his friends, Bill Hooks and Vernon Ford, were born on the Franklin Hill.

Jim Whittington's education continued outside of the classroom, where he learned how to be one with nature by picking or chopping cotton and pulling rostnears. He became a crack shot with rifle, shotgun, and slingshot. He learned how to raise and dress out chickens, milk cows, slaughter hogs; however, the sixth grade marked the end of his public education.

Chapter 6

Visits to Uncle Cliff and Aunt Laurie's

From time to time, the Whittington family would take a trip to Stanly County to visit Eva's eldest son Clifford, Pappy's half-brother. Uncle Cliff owned a hundred acres of land that stretched from McLester Road to Stony Run Creek. Cliff married Laura in 1920. Their farm was about thirty miles from the Franklin Mill, and I can't imagine how long it would have taken the family to make that trip in those days.

If they walked, it would have taken most of the day, and I am sure the route was quite different from the roads that we took. Uncle Cliff's cousin, Vitas, lived just on the other side of McLester Road, and Vitas Honeycutt's property extended up the north side of Bull Hill.

When the Whittingtons visited, they stayed in an old three-room wooden shack located between McLester Road and Stony Run Creek. Pap called this the old place or the old homestead, which was built before the Civil War. The chimney of this house was made of flint rocks.

Pappy told another story while working around the old place, when he was about eleven. One summer day he happened to be carrying buckets of water from the spring to the house. What he didn't know was that his brother Will started shooting into a hornet's nest about a half mile away down by the creek.

Suddenly, he saw something coming straight for his forehead at a high rate of speed, like a slingshot rock. Pappy froze in his footsteps, and by the time he recognized it was a mad hornet coming straight at him, it was too late. He saw the hornet change ends and proceeded to fly tail first until the hornet zeroed in and smashed full force into Pappy's forehead. The jolt knocked him off his feet and caused him to spill both buckets of water.

He had to go back to the spring to refill the buckets. He found out later that Will had shot the nest and gave his brother a verbal browbeating. It didn't do much good because the hornets had stung Will all over, and Uncle Will was in great pain. Uncle Will pledged that he would never do anything that stupid ever again.

Stony Run Creek is where the youngsters would set hooks to catch catfish and small bream (pronounced brim) or hunt squirrels along the banks of the creek. Setting hooks was nothing more than baiting a line connected to a cane pole that you stuck in the bank and left overnight. Pappy, along with others, swore that there were things to be seen and heard around Black Log Lake. In other words, the place was haunted. Black Log Lake happened to be the widest portion of the creek, where two big logs were used as a bridge. These logs spanned the creek so mules, cattle, or people could cross.

One night Pap spent the night across the creek at a friend's house. He was awakened because the bedbugs started biting him, so he decided to return to the old place. On his trip back home, as soon as he stepped onto those logs, something on the other side jumped out on the logs and blocked his path. He said whatever it was had two big red eyes that were staring right at him. He thought it was an old pig, and he stomped his foot on the logs and yelled, "Get outta here!"

The thing on the other end didn't budge but slowly started moving toward him. He dove off the logs into the creek and swam to the other side. After he climbed out on Uncle Cliff's side of the creek, he made it to the old place in record-breaking time.

On another night, as cousin Vitas was returning from a square dance, he looked down on those logs as he topped the bank and swore that there in the moonlight stood the devil himself. Uncle Cliff told me there were times when you could hear a man moaning by the rock quarry a little farther up the creek toward Highway 24.

I always thought they were just pulling my leg; however, I noticed that whenever it started to get dark, they would not tarry around the creek, especially the Black Log Lake area. Finally, during one summer visit, when I was about eight years old, Aunt Laurie and I happened to be breaking beans underneath the big pear tree in the front yard, so I asked her what she thought. I knew she wouldn't steer me wrong.

She was sitting in a chair, wearing a white bonnet; she paused long enough to spit out some of her Tube Rose Snuff then proceeded to tell me about the incident of Stony Run Creek. She said, "A little after the civil war, Alec Whitley and Bud Cagle got into a fight just on the other side of creek. They found Bud's headless body the next day by Black Log Lake. They didn't know whether his head was chopped off by an ax or it was beaten off with a sledgehammer because they never found his head.

"After Alec Whitley killed Bud Cagle, he went home, cut his wife's and children's throats, and threw their bodies into the well. Whitley lit out, and they finally caught up with him somewhere in Missouri, after shooting him in the shoulder."

She went on to say, "They carried him back to Oakboro, had a quick trial, took him out back, hung him, and shot him to pieces." She added, "They cut him down but left the rope as a reminder to what would happen if anyone tried to do anything like that again."

She remembered seeing part of that rope still dangling there when she was a little girl. This was much worse than the Tom Dooley incident that happened near Statesville.

I remember visiting Uncle Cliff's place, which was another world, a young boy's utopia. Uncle Cliff had milk and beef cattle, chickens, pigs, two mules, and untold quantities of rabbits, squirrels, quail, and snipe. When you visited his place, time seemed to stand still. If a visitor entered Uncle Cliff's guest bedroom, they would have noticed an elegant room. I never got to sleep in this room because Uncle Cliff said I drooled too much, and if I had a nightmare, he was afraid I might tear something up.

The bed was one of those four-poster types, draped with colorful quilts made by Aunt Laurie's own hands. On the other side of this bed was a beautiful old wooden light brown radio which came up to my chest. The radio had two big tuning knobs on each side of a huge dial indicator. On special nights, we would listen to a nearby radio station in Albemarle. In my mind, the radio station seemed to be a thousand miles away.

At the foot of the bed, the guest would be astounded by the magnificent dark brown wooden dresser that contained three sections of mirrors outlined in dark Mahogany. This dresser was complete with a small shelf that extended in front of the mirrors. On the left side of this shelf stood a dark brown wind-up clock that had a very pronounced tick, and the alarm would gong every hour. At first, this clock would keep me up at night until I got used to the sound. The clock had to be wound almost every day, and this clock had two places to insert the large brass key to accomplish this task. Uncle Cliff never let me wind the clock; that was his job. After I returned home, I would miss the sound of that old clock.

The most nostalgic item on the other side of the shelf was an oval black and white photo of Cliff in his doughboy uniform, complete with distinctive leggings and his campaign hat. When I studied his picture, it was hard for me to imagine that he was ever that young. By the time of my visit, my uncle was probably around seventy years old. Seeing that picture was a great history lesson, one not covered in any book but was evident in all the things around me. Through history, everything is connected, and when you were at Uncle Cliff's, it was like visiting a historic home; this was real country. You might spend the whole day without seeing or hearing a car pass by.

When the Whittington family came to visit, Pappy would help with the work on Cliff's farm. If there was a layoff in the mill or a sickness in the family, the Whittingtons would stay at Uncle Cliff's. Uncle Will and Pappy were sent from time to time to work the farm when they were out of school.

When I was there, Uncle Cliff had a buckboard wagon, which was pulled by two work mules, which could pull loads almost as heavy as what a three-quarter-ton pickup truck could pull today. He had many head of dairy and beef cattle, a two-story barn down by the spring, two chicken houses, two large pecan trees, a grove of apple and pear trees, and a large scupinine vine. In the back of their house, they had a woodshed and a small building where Aunt Laurie stored grain and canned goods.

The washroom was at the end of an adjacent building, where they cleaned hogs, wild game, or dressed chickens.

Chapter 7

Working at the Franklin

The year 1927 was quite significant. Charles Lindbergh flew nonstop across the Atlantic; the New York Yankees swept the Pittsburgh Pirates in four games during the '27 World Series; Babe Ruth hit sixty homeruns; and two semipro North Carolina Textile baseball teams, the Kannapolis Towlers and the Concord Weavers, squared off at Webb Field in Concord to settle the score between seasonal rivals. It just so happened that James Howard Hooks and Bill Ford were born on the Franklin Mill Hill that year.

September of that year happened to be Jim Whittington's thirteenth birthday. He started working as a helper at the Franklin Mill. Many cotton mill workers started at a young age since a minimum age requirement didn't exist at the time. The minimum age increased to sixteen years in 1938, as part of the federal wage and tax laws that also established the forty-hour workweek. For many, going to work full time in the mills marked the end of their public education.

I could only imagine what Pap thought of the Franklin Mill on his first day on the job. He would have been amazed at seeing three floors of electric belt-driven machines that included opening-room pickers, hoppers, cards, rib-lappers, slubbers, and spinning machines. This would have been like unearthing an indigenous subculture. He would have been able to associate the sounds he had heard outside the mill with the frequency and the hum of a particular machine.

He would not have been assigned to a specific job as a helper but would have to assist a different person every other day and work different machines in various sections. He learned and understood the overall process in the mill in only a few months.

The raw slabs of cotton would have come in one door and was subjected to various machines before the finished product was loaded on a boxcar out the back door for the products to continue the process for completion. The Franklin Mill never had a dyeing process or weaving looms, so the Franklin's finished product was sent to the weave room at the Gibson Mill or Plant 1 in Kannapolis by rail.

There would have been a beehive of human activity on all floors; it would have looked like a fog was forming in each room because of all the cotton dust. The workers carried their meals in brown paper bags called a lunch poke. Most of the workers' shirts would have been stained with sweat, especially under their armpits. The workers usually had two face cloths in their back pockets: One was used for wiping sweat off their faces, and the other was used to blow the cotton dust out of their noses. Those face cloths were manufactured by the Cannon Mill Company.

Most of the men chewed Apple or Brown Mule plug tobacco, and a lot of women dipped Tube Rose Snuff to prevent the dry mouth taste they called cotton mouth. Things like masks, hearing and eye protection, would not have even come onto the textile scene until 1976 in most of the mills. Had a modern-day Occupational Safety and Health Administrator, (OSHA) inspector walked in the Franklin Mill in 1927, that inspector might have suffered a nervous breakdown right there on the spot.

The mill positions included helpers, sweepers, and hands who worked certain machines named as to what type machine they ran, i.e., slubber or card hands. The doffers would move the cotton products from one machine to another type of machine in the process, whenever the wooden bobbins or cans filled up.

Each section had oilers or fixers who were specialized to make a particular set of machines perform up to par. The foreman would have been a section boss, the foremen worked under a shift supervisor, the shift supervisors worked for an overseer, and the superintendent was responsible for the operation of the entire mill.

Some mill workers poked fun at the new-hires, but there was one slubber hand who sort of took my father under his wing and tried to show him the ropes. Mr. Frank was quite older than Pap, and Pappy said he loved to fish, and on many occasions, Mr. Frank would invite him to fish the local creeks and ponds.

For some unexplainable reason, Mr. Frank called my father Pete. Pappy's mentor was a good man, well respected, and somewhat feared by the other workers because he would not hesitate to fight and was quite handy with a pocketknife. If someone angered Mr. Frank, there was a good chance that they might get cut.

One day Mr. Frank came up to Pappy and said, "Pete, it's kind of slow today, let's knock off early and go fishin."

So they left work early that day and walked the short distance to Mr. Frank's mill house. When they stepped up on Mr. Frank's front porch, Pappy heard a woman making noises. Those feminine sounds coming through that mill house bedroom window was either a woman in pain or she was having the time of her life. It was not understood if Pap knew about the facts of life at the time, but he did know something was wrong. The woman making those noises happened to be Mr. Frank's wife, and it was evident that she was not alone. Mr. Frank turned to Pappy and said, "Pete, stay out here on the front porch, and I will come back outside later with the fishing poles."

Pappy felt like he was standing out on that porch for an eternity, not knowing what was going to happen.

A few moments later, Mr. Frank opened the front door, handed Pap a fishing pole, and said, "The fish are waitin' on us."

Pappy was puzzled and really didn't know what went on inside and surmised that his fishing partner had killed the two people inside the house. While walking to their fishing spot, Mr. Frank noticed that Pete was worried and was acting a little nervous at this point, so he gave an explanation. He said, "Pete, when I entered the room, I could see that my wife's lover was scared, so I walked over to the edge of the bed and pulled a dollar out of my bill fold and handed it to him. I told him to take that money and go down to Green Valley and get him a real piece of ass. Then I told my old lady, 'I'm going fishin' with my buddy, Pete, and you better be long gone by the time I get back.'"

Jim Whittington's entry into the textile world was simultaneous with his introduction into the world of organized baseball. There were many mills in the area, and most mills had baseball teams. Some mills had their own baseball fields that consisted of only a backstop, without any type of fence or wall, like the Norcott and Cabarrus mills' ball fields. The Gibson Mill (Plant 6) shared Webb Field with Concord's high school baseball team.

Horseracing, boxing, and baseball dominated the American sports world at the time, even though football, basketball and tennis had been around for quite some time. The attitude toward the early baseball players in 1927 was not very positive. Many of the workers would have wondered why a band of grown-ups would waste so much time when they could have been working in the mills or the fields. They were referred to as deadbeats or bums in pajamas. My grandparents would not have understood ballplayers at all.

In 1919, the Black Sox scandal gave baseball a black eye that left a bad taste in the spectators' mouths for many years. It took the hitting prowess of Babe Ruth to pull baseball out of this social stigma. This attitude toward baseball was starting to change because additional money could be made, and special favors were granted to the ballplayers who played for the mill, even though the textile league was considered semipro.

Chapter 8

Running Slubbers and Playing Baseball

Over the next few years, Jim Whittington exceled in his new profession, and by 1928, he had learned how to operate many different machines. He could keep up and even outproduce most of the grown-ups, but his favorite machines were the slubbers.

A slubber frame was a machine about fifty feet long with two rows of spindles, an inner row and an outer row, which were spaced in an offset position to facilitate doffing the spindles. A wooden bobbin about twelve to fifteen inches long would be seated on the metal spindle, and the bobbin would be held in place as the outer spindle or flyer would thread the bobbin. There would be about forty to fifty spindles to each slubber frame.

The slubbers would receive the finished product that came from the card machines. The cards transformed a slab of cotton that was fed into one side of the machine, and the cotton that came out of the back of this machine was a like a rope of cotton about a half inch to an inch in diameter. These strands would be coiled and deposited into cans with a spring attached to the bottom. As those cans filled, the spring would compress, and the bottom of the can would lower to the floor. These cans were about chest high and about two feet in diameter. Anytime a can, bobbin, or box was filled, the machine would be shut down, and the finished can or bobbins would be taken from that machine and replaced with a new container before the machine was restarted. This process was called doffing. After the cans from behind the cards filled, they were moved to the back of the slubbers.

The worker would shut the slubbers down, break the cotton ropes from the cans that were almost empty, and splice or attach that strand to the cotton stored in the full cans. Each spindle had its own can feed from the back of the machine. You never wanted a can to run out in the middle of the process. The slubbers would take the rope-like strands from the card cans, twist and stretch the cotton until it was about three or four times the size of kite string, and wrap that thread onto wooden bobbins. Then the worker would go around to the front of the slubbers and place forty or fifty empty bobbins, so every spindle had an empty bobbin ready to receive the cotton.

The worker would thread or wrap the twine around the new bobbin and place the flyers on top of the spindle and restart the machine. After that person saw that all the bobbins were taking the thread, the worker turned the machine on full blast, and the flyers would spin at high speed.

The machine would shut itself down if there was a malfunction or if the bobbins were full and ready to doff. This process of doffing took place two to three times per shift, per frame, and a slubber hand could have as many as four frames going at a time. A good slubber hand would manage their frames so they would not have to doff two frames at the same time. Their pay was a result of their machines; production.

Everything appeared to be progressing normally in and around Concord with the expansion of the mills. Communities began to thrive in and around those mills. It became a partnership between the old world and the new.

Pappy and his buddies were growing up and played more intense backyard baseball. They occasionally went to see the adults play on the non-lighted, fenceless ball fields at the Norcott, Cabarrus, and Roberta baseball fields. Most of these young mill hillers never received any formal training, like I did on the baseball field; they just mimicked their favorite ballplayers then tried out their new tactics against one another.

Many of the young players volunteered to shag or chase down balls that were hit out of play or over the fence. Webb, Winecoff, and the Brown mills fields were the only ball fields that had fences. While chasing balls, Pappy was in direct competition with the Mauney boys, who were faster than greased lightning. The one who snagged the ball first would achieve a small victory. The grown-ups who played at the time were thankful that the ball chasers were available because baseballs were not cheap, and money didn't grow on trees. Some of those ballplayers rewarded those young athletes the best they could by giving them an old bat or by letting them keep the water-logged balls they retrieved out of the creek. Some would play catch with the boys after the game, while others might get to try on the catching gear. Even the most notorious and hotheaded adult ballplayers had a soft spot for those youngsters.

Thirty-seven years later, I found myself shagging and returning baseballs hit into Three Mile Branch along Webb Field or chasing softballs hit into foul territory from Macalister Field. I was rewarded 10¢ a ball, so after retrieving several balls, I could treat myself to a concession-stand snow cone or a hot dog after the game. Ball chasers didn't have to pay an admission fee, and I could see the ball games being played on two different fields at the same time.

This ball-chasing activity took place around thousands of other ball fields throughout America. Although not noticed by the public, this sideline action took place from the time baseball was in its infant stage and still flourishes to this day.

Jim Whittington happened to be one of the ball chasers totally fascinated with the game, and by doing so, he met his catching mentor, Herman Ginger Watts at Webb Field. Herman Ginger Watts, a local legendary ballplayer and a catcher. Ginger Watts gave Pap his first lesson by showing him how to don the catching gear, how to position himself behind the plate, and how to give signals to the pitcher. Ginger Watts happened to light a prairie fire in Pap's twelve-year old heart. The bond established between those two that day continued throughout the remainder of their lives. Pappy found mentorship in others when he could not find it in his own family. There is no secret in this: All a youngster wants is for someone to show them something, and this goes a long way.

Chapter 9

The Crash

The song "The Big Rock Candy Mountains," written by Henry Mclintock in 1928, reflected a hobo's perspective of utopia, which indicated that there were hard times and earlier recessions before most people realize. Homeless travelers hitched rides and stowed away on or underneath boxcars to travel to other locations from 1893 through the early 1920s.

Then suddenly, there was breaking news in the papers and from the lips of most throughout the country, when the stock market crashed on October 29, 1929. This day became known as Black Tuesday. Most economists use this to mark the beginning of the Great Depression, which at the time was called the Crash of '29. Fear and panic prevailed, fortunes were lost, and banks began to fold.

President Hoover and his administration were blamed for the phenomena, just like presidents are blamed today for things beyond their control. Jobless and homeless people congregated in shantytowns called Hoovervilles. Cars that were pulled by horses, because the owners could not afford gas, were known as Bennett buggies or Hoover wagons. Empty pockets turned inside out were known as Hoover flags. The unemployment rate skyrocketed;

droves of jobless people began to pile onto trains to try to find some type of work. The country had just gone to hell financially.

Although North Carolina was hit hard, it fared better than the Midwestern states because of its agricultural base and the stability the cotton mill barons provided. Despite this economic upheaval, this activity became sort of a blessing for the mill workers and local baseball players.

The people on the hill were worried because nothing like this had ever been experienced, but because of their resilience and tenacity, they were able to weather the Great Depression somewhat better than others. There were several reasons why North Carolina fared better than other states.

The first was these textile workers were dirt poor and didn't have any fortunes to lose. At the time, an oiler in the mill made about $20-23 a paycheck for ten days of work. Workers didn't have any money to deposit into the bank. If the local banks collapsed, so what? Charlie Cannon was very wealthy and provided financial stability by backing local banks and kept the surrounding counties and the state of North Carolina afloat during those troubled times.

Those workers did not have any homes to lose because they lived in mill houses. Most farming families inherited houses where the mortgages were already paid; however, if a family lost their house or was out of work, they moved in with a relative until they found work or got back on their feet financially.

The large farming areas that exported crops were adversely affected by the Smoot-Hawley Tariff Act of 1930, which raised the prices of exported crops because of foreign retaliation to the act. The local farmers stopped exporting and sold their products locally. The common sense, goodwill, and wisdom of the local farmers saved many communities. Local farmers would show up in the streets of many mill hills and other localities, pulling wagons filled with baskets or buckets of corn, cucumbers, tomatoes, squash, green beans, and peas. They sold their goods door-to-door. There were enough hungry people around, and this blessing was viewed as a gift from God.

Unlike the Midwestern states, the Carolina farmers were not plagued with a five-year drought, nor were they afflicted with huge dust storms that choked and killed people as well as their crops. However, crop prices did drop significantly. The people in and around Concord and Cabarrus County held their breath and knew things might even get worse.

The Depression hurt Major League Baseball and its farm system because salaries were significantly reduced. Major League Baseball at the time was known as the National Association of Professional Baseball or NAPBL. The farm system structure that supported the NAPBL had five different levels: AA or A1, A, B, C, and D levels.

Contrary to popular belief, a ballplayer who was contracted to play D level or above was a professional baseball player, which included a signed contract with salary and conditions. A professional player could not play at a lower level or for another organization or even compete at the amateur level unless he was released from that contract.

Many of the textile mills, especially in the Piedmont region, had baseball teams; there were at least twelve different mills in Concord alone. Although there were good ballplayers coming out of high schools and Carolina colleges, the school system during that time frame was not structured like today because only a few could afford a college education.

The majority of ballplayers were recruited from the Carolina Textile Baseball Leagues. Textile baseball could be considered the farm system for the Minor Leagues, and those Minor League managers knew where their bread was buttered.

The conditions were right; the stage was set for the meteoric rise of baseball, especially in the Piedmont region of North Carolina. The economic stability of the textile industry, plus the volume of players and popularity of the national sport, provided a new look, fueled by the damage caused to the farm teams by the Depression. This gave rise to a local phenomenon, where amateur baseball players could make money doing something they loved.

It worked to the mill owners' advantage to stack their baseball teams with the best talent possible. This worked out well for the mill because fans wanted to see their local baseball stars perform, and they rooted for their mill teams. Textile teams were considered semipro, a term frequently used but very few understood what this label really meant.

A semiprofessional ballplayer is almost a contradiction of terms, a misnomer. In reality, a player is either a professional or an amateur. However, the company mill or industrial league teams provided a means where a nonprofessional ballplayer could be paid to play and still maintain amateur status.

A semipro contract was a verbal agreement with the worker's supervisors, giving the worker full/partial pays, fringe benefits, or special favors, as long as that person played for that particular team. This was the way mill teams stacked baseball teams.

This was commonly practiced at the amateur level; local businessmen and leading citizens knew that these methods could be exercised at the professional level as well. This was understood as before the Depression. Because of the fall of the stock market on Black Tuesday, the Depression hit the baseball Minor Leagues so hard. Professional ballplayers had to be cut loose or their pay so restricted, which resulted in ballplayers all across the country to look for alternative means or ways to showcase their talent and make a living. They found that alternative right around Concord, when the Independent Carolina Baseball League was formed. This turned North Carolina into a baseball mecca.

Chapter 10

Jim Becomes Shad Rack

Father's interaction with his playmates started taking on a new direction, and he honed his competitive skills with those within the neighborhood on and around the Franklin Mill.

One must realize that through this camaraderie was how these boys and young men learned how to master the game of baseball. There were many games played among the boys on the hill, and being that play time was so limited, they had to make their play time count.

Like the Mauney and Lefler families, baseball was first played among the siblings of the family group. Those ballplayers would have competed with one another, and each would have to trade off and play all the positions. In other words, every player would have to pitch, catch, or change positions many times during a game. There may be only one guy playing the left side of the infield between second and third and another family member playing first and second base with maybe one or two outfielders. This was the same way my contemporaries played whiffle ball in the early '60s.

Through this amalgamation, it would have been understood within that family unit who was the better outfielder, catcher, or pitcher. And each of these ballplayers learned to hit and hit well.

However, it would have been to the boy's advantage to include additional players outside the family circle to round out or fill an entire team. No hitter in baseball wants to chase after a ball that he just hit, that only happens in golf, so an entire defense is desired.

There were enough youngsters on the Franklin hill to form at least two teams, and if not, they only had to go across 29A, on the Hartsell Mill Hill, to find another team. This activity was happening the same time those boys' fathers were playing against the other mill teams at the adult level.

By the time my father's generation was old enough to play men's level baseball, they had been playing many years at this unstructured tier and were well versed at the game. It must be understood that the Little League, Babe Ruth, or the high school structured organizations available to my generation were not available to those mill hillers.

Jim Whittington threw right-handed but was a left-handed hitter. When he was fifteen years old, he had already received notoriety as a good hitter. By this time, he had been playing on the Franklin, Hartsell, Cabarrus, and Norcott mills hills. His exceptional eyesight, excellent hand-and-eye coordination, quick wrists, and deep concentration made it hard for pitchers to get him out. It didn't hurt in the least that he caught most of the pitchers around the area, so he got to see how those pitchers worked, learned what pitch they would throw in the clutch, but mainly, he knew how they thought.

Other hitting assets included the lack of a hitch found in his swing; his movement was only toward the pitch. He stood in an upright stance, held his bat straight back across his shoulder, so when he swung, that swing was level. When he hit the ball, his power was generated from his back foot, through his hips, and transferred that power to the fat part of the bat.

He swung the bat with tremendous bat speed and did not grip the bat before the pitch was delivered, but gripped the bat as he swung. When he swung, you could hear the bat whistle. His swing was so fast you could not follow the bat with the natural eye, which proved to be rough for infielders trying to catch the balls he hit. When Pappy came up to bat, the infielders would naturally take a few steps back.

These assets made him an exceptional hitter, and regardless of his five-feet-nine-inch thin, lean frame at the time, he could hit towering home runs, even at a young age. He had an inside-out or could adjust to an outside-in swing, depending on where the pitch was thrown. This enabled him to hit an outside pitch to the opposite field, down the left-field line, as well as pull the ball into right-field if the pitch was inside. He called this "hitting the ball where it was pitched."

Most of the ball fields he played on in 1931 were open fields, and only Brown and Webb fields had fences. By this time, he had already developed quite a fan following. When he stepped up to the plate, some of the fans would shout, "Here comes the Rack!" This meant he was going to rack up some runs.

When playing at Roberta Ball Field one day and after hitting one into the woods during his next visit to the plate, the fans started yelling to the outfielders, "You better get back in the shade!" They were telling the outfielders to play at the edge of the woods, underneath the shade of the trees.

The same thing happened when he played on the Cabarrus Mill ballpark by the depot in Concord, especially when the summer cornstalks were about seven feet high.

This term, *shade,* changed over time and was shortened to "shad." The two names were combined, and he became known as Shad Rack. Many would think that his nickname had a biblical connotation, but this was not the case. Pappy told me the fans gave him his baseball name, and this name stuck with him throughout his life. There were many people in the area who never knew his real name. They called him Shad or Shad Rack.

During the '31 baseball season, a Cincinnati talent scout noticed Pappy and had a talk with him after the game. The scout wanted to sign him to a baseball contract, but Pap was still a minor, so they arranged for the scout to meet his mom and discuss the contract. Pap knew that if they approached Bud Whittington, he would be difficult to deal with and would probably run the talent scout out of his yard. So

Pap invited this man to his house on the Franklin Mill Hill to meet his mom, Eva Whittington. Pappy's dream was about to come true.

The meeting commenced, and Grandmother listened intently as this scout described the terms and conditions of the contract, but she remained silent throughout the presentation.

When it came down to the signing of the contract, Grandmother looked at the man and said sternly, "I am not selling my boy."

The man reiterated and explained, "No, Mrs. Whittington, you are not selling your boy, he will just work for us and come back home after the season is over."

Eva stood up and said, "I told you, I am not selling my boy," and then she got up and went back into the house.

Pap's dream was crushed. He knew his mom didn't know anything about baseball, but there was nothing he could do or say about it.

Well, Eva told her husband about the meeting after he got off work, and Bud Whittington flew into a tirade and tore my father's ass up for what he had done. In other words, he whipped him hard. After this happened, Pappy decided to run away from home that night.

After the sun went down, Pappy slipped out of the house and walked down to the train depot in front of the Cabarrus Mill. He decided to jump on a freight train and never come back. Somehow he found out that this particular train was bound for Del Rio, Texas, and that was far enough away for him. He found a blind spot on the train and climbed on top a boxcar and met another young lad on top of this boxcar with the same idea. They had evaded the railroad dicks that were checking the boxcars, and as the train started its slow departure out of Concord, they were Texas-bound. As Father stated many times during his life, "They had the world by the ass."

Little did the potential runaways know that the railroad companies were very professional and had unique ways of catching and convincing non-ticketed passengers there were no free rides. The Depression had been in effect for about twenty-two months, and the railroad men had plenty of practice in dislodging unwanted passengers.

After the train pulled away from Concord, it started to pick up speed, and the two passengers were caught off guard when they heard the brakeman behind them yell, "Jar the ground!"

Those boys were shocked. Their eyes appeared to be as wide-eyed as two owls after they saw the railroad man dressed in a dark uniform eased closer to them. The boys held their breath after they noticed he was carrying a large hammer in his hand, ready for action. The railroad dick said, "You have a choice: jump off or I will knock you off."

They decided to jump.

Pappy jumped first, and his buddy was right behind him. Pappy hit the ground so hard it knocked the wind out of him. He tumbled down a valley, rolled up a bank, and ended up in a green briar patch, probably the worst day of his life up to this point. He was cut up pretty bad but not seriously hurt. Soon afterward, Pap found his injured stowaway buddy; they bade each other goodbye and parted ways.

Nothing more was said after Pappy got back home to Robinson Street. Only a half a month later, twenty-three days before Pap's seventeenth birthday, the Japanese invaded Manchuria.

Chapter 11

Radio on the Hill

Pappy, like many others during this generation, started smoking at a young age. Several mill hillers smoked short grapevine stems or rolled their homemade blend of Rabbit Tobacco. Cigarettes were referred to as coffin nails as early as 1931. He also indulged in taking snorts of whisky and beer. Cabarrus County was a wet county and bars could were not far from the Franklin Mill.

One was located between the Hartsell Mill and Hartsell School; the other bar run by Mr. Yates was beside the intersection of Roberta Road and Highway 29A, known today as the old Charlotte Highway. The bar near Hartsell School was too close to home, so he visited the bar along 29A. He was unfamiliar with this environment but wanted to study the wildlife that frequented the place. Everybody knew he was underaged, but if you had money for beer and behaved yourself, no questions were asked.

Along with the drinking and carousing that took place on Friday and Saturday nights, about four or five of the regulars played poker over in the far corner of this establishment. Two of the gamblers were WW1 veterans. One carried a sharp pocketknife, and the other packed a .38 special underneath his jacket. Both men had quick tempers and hated to lose in anything, especially money in a poker game.

While Pappy was sipping his beverage, the entire place turned silent when the knife-carrying vet accused the other veteran of cheating and said in a loud voice, "I caught you cheatin', dammit. I have a good notion to stick you in the gut and walk around you a couple of times."

After hearing this, the accused man pushed his chair back a little and said, "If you take a step toward me, you will tell Saint Peter what you did wrong."

The accuser took that step, and then everyone heard a deafening pistol blast.

Pappy squeezed out through a little circular window, and people in the bar got out as fast as they could, their ears still ringing from the gunshot. That shot killed the fellow. The shooter was caught, arrested, and hauled off to jail the same night. Pappy returned a few nights later and could not squeeze through the window opening he had exited so easily during the shooting. That was the last time he visited this place when it was still a bar.

By this time, many of the mill houses had radios, and they could listen to local and world news. Franklin Delano Roosevelt, elected president in 1932, was known as the first radio president. He delivered radio messages called Fireside Chats. Those radio messages gave the people hope in the midst of desperation and despair.

Those mill hillers and others across the nation tuned in regularly to hear their new president speak. The president's ebullient inaugural speech caught their attention when he said, "All we have to fear is fear itself."

The people of that period also learned about programs such as the National Industrial Recovery Act (NIRA), the Civilian Conservation Corps (CCC), and the Work Progress Administration(WPA).

President Roosevelt asked the people for their help and for suggestions or critiques and ways to improve the system. One older gentleman who worked at the Franklin stated, "That is the first time the president of the United States ever asked for my advice, he is okay in my book."

Pretty soon, that word spread throughout the mill, and other workers said, "That man is right."

The year 1933 was when the Depression reached its lowest point in America. Radio listeners also heard about a fellow by the name of Adolph Hitler, who had just become Germany's new chancellor.

The Three Stooges made their movie debut in 1934 and were Pappy's favorite. I think he learned most of his vocabulary from watching the Three Stooges. He began to echo terms like *nitwit*, *numbskull*, *half-wit*, and *lame-brained* on and off the ball field. Although the Stooges became an instant movie hit, radio remained the king of media for quite some time.

Other radio broadcasts included *Amos 'n' Andy*, *Gang Busters*, and T*he Lone Ranger.* Radio listeners were not glued to a television set, and as long as they were within earshot of the radio, they could do things around the house and not miss out. The listener had to use their imagination as to what the performers might have looked like or how they were performing.

The mill hillers were astounded on May 23, 1934, when they heard that Clyde Chestnut Barrow and Bonnie Elizabeth Parker were cut down by a fusillade of gunfire by the Frank Hamer-led posse in Bienville Parish, near Gibsland, Louisiana.

Less than two months later, those listeners were shocked even more when they heard that John Dillinger, public enemy number one, was taken by surprise and shot outside the Biograph Theater by Melvin Purvis's men in Chicago. This was the first time they even heard about the Federal Bureau of Investigation.

Local news worried the mill workers concerning the "Great Textile Mill Strike of '34," which took place twenty-six days before Pap's twentieth birthday. The workers' hours were cut in the mills. Section 7a of the National Industrial Recovery Act promoted the organization of labor unions. Because of this cutback in hours, picket lines formed just outside the Franklin Mill gate, and union organizers tried to stop the mill workers from going to work. The union men cussed the mill workers and called them scabs, while the workers filed into work.

This led to violent confrontations, and fights broke out near the gates. Those union organizers failed to realize that very few workers, if any, had lost their jobs during this downturn or were turned out of their mill houses. If a mill worker went on strike, they would not only lose their jobs, but would have been turned out of their mill houses as well.

The mill owners didn't want to have a repeat of the Loray Mill unrest experienced in Gaston County in 1929. In the 1934 strike, Kannapolis strikers faced two military companies, aided by additional deputy sheriffs carrying shotguns. A resident of the Franklin Mill area stated that the National Guard was called in, and a machine gun was placed on top of the mill, and a curfew was enforced. This scenario was mirrored around other textile communities in the area.

Ethel Marie and Jim (Shad) Whittington at Coley Airport circa 1935. The Coley Airport discontinued service in the mid-1950s. The property later became Fleetwood shopping and housing area, also known as Stop & Shop.

Chapter 12

Shad Meets Ethel Marie

Pappy was quite taken by a young lady who worked in the spinning room on the first shift. She was an attractive brunette with shoulder-length brown hair that filled out a five-foot-six curvy frame. He started talking to her almost every day. Pretty soon they were seen taking their breaks together and talking more in depth about things in general.

They started dating in 1935, which included taking a walk to one of the many theaters in Concord to watch a movie or by visiting Coley Airport along Union Cemetery Road. One of the few pictures taken of the couple was at this airport, beside a bi-winged aircraft. The airport was located on the north side of Union Cemetery Road, where Fleetwood housing area stands today.

When their shift was over, they decided to walk downtown to watch a movie that was playing at one of the theaters on Union Street. Theaters were quite plentiful in Concord, and it took a while for the couple to make up their minds. They had a choice between *Captain Blood*, the new Errol Flynn movie, showing at the Standard; or the Gary Cooper film, *The Lives of a Bengal Lancer*, showing at the Cabarrus Theater. They chose the Gary Cooper film because they didn't know this Errol Flynn fellow and could come back on another date to see *Captain Blood*.

After Shad bought two movie tickets, two fountain Cokes, and a small bucket of popcorn, they settled in to watch the movie. This dating adventure would have amounted to about three hours of work in the mill. They enjoyed their outing at the Cabarrus Theater that evening, and as they walked back home, they agreed to see other movies in the future.

Brother Ted took me to my first walk-in movie twenty-seven years later, when I was eight years old. The movie was *Jack the Giant Killer*, featured in 1962 at the same theater. In 1962, a dime bought a movie ticket, a nickel for a fountain Coke, and a dime for a box of Cracker Jacks, which usually had some sort of prize inside the box: a total of 25¢.

A production mill worker's salary in 1962 was about a dollar an hour, and two people could enjoy a movie and refreshments in '62 and spend a half hour's worth of one's wages. Although the prices were quite different from 1935 to 1962, the one constant was if you were a baseball player scheduled to play a day game, it was taboo to watch a movie before a game. It messed your eyes up and hampered your hitting ability; however, playing at night was not a problem.

Pappy skipped baseball practice to take Ethel to the movies. Normally, nothing on the planet would have kept him away from the ball field, but she was very important. The mill teams played scheduled games on Wednesday evenings and Saturday mornings. The Franklin Mill during this time would close down after the second shift finished work on Friday and reopen again Monday morning.

The mill company designed and built the Franklin Mill ballpark between the north side of the railroad tracks and south of Zion Church Road, just east of the railroad bridge, where Wilshire Drive crossed over the tracks. This field was laid out with ninety feet between bases, without a fence or a wall in the outfield. There was no mound or ant hill. The pitching rubber was level with the infield, which gave the hitters an advantage. This field was never lighted, so games had to be finished before it got to too dark to see. This ballpark was devoid of bleachers or places for the spectators to sit; fans brought their own chairs, wooden ale crates, or just sat in the grass.

The Franklin field backstop consisted of four sawed-off telephone poles placed into the ground behind home plate, with two strands or layers of chicken wire nailed onto those poles. After several fouled balls or wild pitches hit the backstop, it would start to bulge, and the chicken wire would become weak in that area. The unsuspecting spectators sitting directly behind this bulged patch would be in danger of the next pitch or foul ball piercing the chicken wire and hitting them.

Some balls would stick in the chicken wire; the umpire would call a time out, and someone would go behind the backstop, take a baseball bat, and knock the ball out of the wire back onto the field. If the baseball was still in good shape, it would be thrown back to the pitcher; otherwise, another ball would have to be put in play. Teams only had two or three baseballs for a game, unlike the abundance of baseballs used in today's games.

Many fans would get excited during the game and stick their fingers through the wire. Pap saw foul balls or wild pitches hit their fingers and almost cut them off. So he would warn the fans not to stick their fingers through the wire. Despite Pappy's safety-conscious attitude, I have heard other ballplayers say, "I saw Shad Whittington catch those hard-throwing pitchers without a chest protector or cup. He just wore a catcher's mask and shin guards."

There were three tiers of baseball played at the Franklin ballpark. The first tier or level was where the scrimmage games were played among the mill teams, namely Roberta, Cabarrus, Norcott, Brown, and Gibson mills. Shad Whittington would have been playing at this adult level for at least four seasons by this time.

After the adults' game or practice was finished, the field gave way to the second tier or the next wave of ballplayers. This younger group of ballplayers included names like Richard, Marvin, and Frank Mauney; Vernon Ford; Bill and Howard Hooks: and Conway Foster.

The final tier or group that played on the Franklin was the least known but the most nostalgic. On some Saturdays, the Franklin Mill community played against one another, which included a mix of seasoned and inexperienced ballplayers. The seasoned ballplayers wore their uniforms and steel spikes, while the non-seasoned players dressed however they felt that day. Some went shirtless and wore street shoes, while others played in overalls and work boots. The inexperienced players would have to borrow the other team players' gloves before they went out in the field.

This family outing attracted much larger crowds than the more serious games played among the mill teams. The spectators came dressed in their Sunday best. Men wore their white straw hats or skimmers, complete with white shirts, slacks, and newly shined shoes. The ladies wore nice dresses with stylish bonnets, and wives carried baskets of food they had prepared earlier that day. This Franklin Mill outing was about as rustic as anything Norman Rockwell could paint.

Once both teams had about the best mix of skilled and unskilled players, the more difficult problem was who they would get to umpire the game. There would only be one umpire. Normally, there are two. This position was usually filled from among the seasoned ballplayers. However, those players had to remain neutral and not favor their team when they called the game. The fans wanted the preacher from the Westford Methodist Church to umpire because they believed he was in good with the Lord. Everyone knew if any player acted a fool or showed unsportsmanlike conduct during the game, the preacher might mention that person's name during his sermon on Sunday.

The poor umpire had to use the catcher's equipment, whose team happened to be batting at the time, and would change gear with the other catcher when the sides changed; a common practice even in the mill leagues when there was only one umpire available. If the umpire didn't want to bother wearing the equipment, he could pick a spot slightly behind and on one side of the pitcher and call the game from that position.

Hulan Lefler was the starting pitcher for one team, and his brother James, a.k.a. Snake, pitched for the other team. Hulan's mother had baked a cake the night before, which was to be the trophy that would be presented to the most outstanding player of the day. The pitchers and catchers were regular ballplayers.

When a seasoned hitter came up to bat, they pitched to that hitter like they would in a regular game, but if an unskilled person came up to bat, the pitchers threw the ball easy so they could hit.

The game was quite comical, especially when an inexperienced player did something out of the ordinary, like run to third base after he hit the ball or run around in a circle when trying to catch a pop fly, which brought everybody to their knees in laughter, especially among the veteran players. People really didn't care about the final score or who won. It was games like these which made baseball the national pastime.

A little ceremony was held after the game, where Mrs. Lefler, Hulan's mom, presented her wonderfully baked cake to Shoddy Mac Ford, called SM, Bill and Vernon Ford's older uncle. SM received the award after hitting a tremendous home run so far out in the field that the outfielders just quit chasing the ball, and SM started walking as he rounded third base on his way to home.

As Shad walked Ethel back to her house, they talked about all the funny things that happened, and he could see she really enjoyed the game. Shad told his girl that he would see her after he got his haircut and cleaned up at Heath Simpson's Barbershop. The barbershop was located in one of the lower rooms of the Franklin Mill. Heath and his brother John were the two Franklin barbers.

The shop had two chairs and a potbellied stove to heat the room and the water because this was the only place that a regular mill worker could take a hot shower. A customer could get a haircut, a straight-razor shave, and a shower. Sometimes the customers could be entertained by the Franklin Mill Band that rehearsed in the room upstairs during their visit.

When Shad, all spruced up, left the barbershop, he walked over to Ethel's house, ready for another date. The attraction between the two grew stronger, and they were married. Not long after their marriage, they moved into a mill house on 69 Railroad Street and shared the home with Carl and Lora Yow. As a nineteen-year-old, Jim Whittington, a productive worker at the Franklin Mill, a prominent baseball player in the Carolina Textile League; now with a wife, a house, ready to start his own family. Things appeared to be going as planned, but troubles started brewing abroad.

A few days after Shad's twentieth birthday, Mussolini riled up his Italian compadres and invaded Ethiopia, but the bad part was that the Italian forces used phosgene and mustard gas to help accomplish this goal. The Italian dictator had plans to reestablish the glory of Rome, but this outbreak of hostility illustrated that the League of Nations was ill-equipped to exercise any oversight. Furthermore, Italy and Ethiopia were members of the League of Nations, adding to the dilemma. This gave the green light for other countries to follow Mussolini's example.

European countries adversely affected by the World Depression, now in its sixth year, were trying to recover from the industrialization of the early '20s. The trauma of WW1 promoted social unrest from the unemployed multitudes, which gave rise to dictatorships.

Back on the mill hill in 1936, Jim and Ethel became the proud parents of a son, James Manual Whittington Jr. Ethel was only fifteen years old at the time. That year also produced the Independent Carolina Baseball League, of which Concord and the surrounding textile communities established their first homegrown class D version of professional baseball. This mix of local businessmen and mill company influence gave rise to a national baseball magnet that attracted ballplayers from all parts of the country because those class D ballplayers were paid at the A League level.

Pappy was the last of the boys to move out of the mill house on Robinson Street. By this time, his eldest brother, Clearance, was living in the rural outskirts of Lincolnton, North Carolina, and married Beulah Mae Christopher. Several years before Pappy moved out, Will left the Robinson Street home and had taken a job at the Roberta Mill. He rented a Roberta mill house after he married Nanny Hooks, who also grew up on the Franklin Mill Hill.

When Shad Whittington was not working or playing ball, he would watch as many games as he could when the Weavers played at Webb Field. By 1936, Webb Field was one of the earliest ball fields around Concord that had lights, so the fans could enjoy night baseball, which meant more spectators and more ticket sales. Games no longer had to be stopped and replayed later because of darkness.

This lesson was learned several years earlier, in 1932, when lights were provided to a Forest City, North Carolina baseball field, courtesy of Branch Rickey. They played so many night games there;

the team was called the Forest City Owls. Forest City had lights before many of the Major League fields were lighted in much larger cities.

The lights on those fields were different from the more advanced lighting fixtures, with the concave reflecting socket and the protective heat-resistant covers that prevailed after WW2 throughout today. Those earlier lights were big incandescent light bulbs without covers. So if a thunderstorm came up or even a light cool rain hit those hot light bulbs, they would explode. Those bulbs cost about $5 each, and this was why the groundkeepers at these lighted fields were told, "If you feel a drop of rain, throw the light switch, even if it is in the middle of a pitch."

Shad took Ethel Whittington to Downtown Concord to watch another movie in December 1936. The couple was faced with a choice between another Gary Cooper film, directed by Frank Capra, and another Errol Flynn movie, *The Charge of the Light Brigade.* They chose the Errol Flynn movie.

Just before the movie started, the Newsreel Movie News came on, featuring the civil war in Spain, which showed Italian and German air forces bombing Spanish civilians. Shad, Ethel, and everyone in the theater wondered what they were doing over there. Shad looked at his wife and said, "Those people act like a bunch of damn nitwits."

People started to take notice of Mussolini by this time.

Some locals treated the other counties, like Mecklenburg and Union counties, as if they were foreign countries. Radio was the instrument that connected them to a world they had never seen, heard of, nor thought they would ever see. There was mention of the 1936 Summer Olympics in Berlin, Germany, where Jessie Owens won the gold in four different track events.

Bud Whittington's health started to decline in the fall of 1936 and could no longer work in the mill, so Bud and Eva left their mill home on Robinson Street and moved to Stanly County to live with Cliff and Laurie at the old place. Less than a year later, William Monroe (Bud) Whittington died of a heart attack in a Charlotte hospital. Uncle Will served as a witness.

In all the years that I knew my father, he never told me any details about Grandfather and hardly spoke about the man. Father never mentioned how he died or where he was buried. Pappy's childhood must have been hell on earth. Yet despite this, Ted Wayne Whittington, Jim and Ethel's second son, was born in the house on 69 Railroad Avenue on January 21, 1938.

FRANKLIN MILL FAST-PITCH SOFTBALL TEAM

Top row L-R: Shad Whittington, Charles Lefler, Hulan Lefler, Leonard Lefler, Luke Mauney, Buck Lefler, Oscar Mincey
2nd row L-R: Marvin Mauney, Leroy Mauney, Jack Grey, Raymond Blackwelder, Floyd Medlin, George Hawkins
1st row L-R: Roy Christenbury, Conway foster, Junior Mincey, David Cooper

Chapter 13

When the Men Played Fast-Pitch

Fast-pitch softball was a prominent game, essentially a cousin to baseball, played in the mid to late '30s and into the mid-'50s within the region. Mills would also sponsor fast-pitch teams, although not as popular or as well documented as baseball was played throughout the region with great intensity.

The fast-pitch season started near the tail end of the baseball season. Some ballplayers played both types of games during the same week. Textile baseball games were played on Wednesday evenings and Saturday mornings. Fast-pitch games were played on Tuesday and Thursday evenings.

The similarities between the two games were that both had nine defensive players in the field, base runners could steal bases, and batters could bunt. Yet the softball was bigger but harder to hit. The softball field dimensions were smaller, with its sixty feet distance between bases, instead of ninety feet in baseball, and the softball field had shorter fences.

A baseball game went nine innings, whereas a fast-pitch game lasted seven innings, as long as the score wasn't tied. The longest baseball bat was thirty-six inches long, and the maximum length of the softball bat was thirty-four inches, with a maximum weight of thirty-eight ounces. The greatest difference between the two games was the way the pitchers delivered the ball, as well as the distance the pitcher was from the catcher.

A baseball pitcher threw the ball overhand or side armed and usually pitched from a small hill or mound, and the distance from the pitcher's rubber to the plate was sixty-feet feet and six inches. The fast-pitch pitcher threw underhand, with a windmill or a slingshot type delivery from only forty-six feet away, which made the fast-pitch softball get to the catcher much faster, and the pitch was much harder to hit.

The game of fast-pitch was more abbreviated, faster, and more difficult for the hitters and the offense to score runs. Most fast-pitch games were usually low-scoring games, and a hit or a walk followed by an error usually equaled a run. Most fast-pitch games were usually won by scoring one or two runs because the pitchers dominated the hitters.

Shad Whittington became one of the premier pitchers in the fast-pitch league. He was paid $5 if he pitched and $10 if he was the winning pitcher. Unlike a baseball pitcher, a fast-pitch pitcher could pitch back-to-back games because the under-armed delivery was more natural. A fast-pitch pitcher could make more money in one night than a baseball pitcher. Fast-pitch was not only fun to play, but it was also another way for the players to make money. A player's pay could be supplemented by the mill he played for; players could be rewarded or tipped, if they unknowingly helped a gambler win a bet. Plenty of side-betting took place during the Great Depression, especially when baseball and fast-pitch softball games were played.

The fast-pitch hitters could hit even better when they switched back to baseball because of the increased distance from the pitcher to the catcher, which gave them much more time to see the ball and react. Fast-pitch hitters didn't have time to take full cuts nor hold their bats down on the end. They usually choked up and just tried to make contact. Hitters who had any type of bad habit, such as a hitch or a hesitation in their swing, would not have appreciated the game of fast-pitch softball.

The pitchers in fast-pitch had two types of deliveries: the windmill or a slingshot type. Fast-pitch pitchers usually had two or three different types of pitches, which included a drop, a rise ball, or a knuckle ball. The good pitchers could change speeds on all those pitches. A drop is a pitch that leaves the pitcher's hand with a forward spin and drops as the spin takes effect. A rise ball or the raise pitch, as it was called then, was an upside-down curve or slider. The knuckle ball was a pitch that did not spin at all but could move erratically in any direction like a butterfly.

During the early days of fast-pitch, the pitcher had additional advantages. He could walk up to the rubber then deliver the pitch, which added to the pitcher's body momentum. The pitcher could swing his arm in a circle multiple times, making the hitter wonder on which cycle the pitcher would release the ball. A pitcher could also throw the ball behind his back to pick off the runner at first base. In the early days of fast-pitch, the runner could lead off the base just like in baseball.

The game changed significantly over time. Now the pitcher has to start his motion with one foot planted firmly on the rubber. Male pitchers could only cross their hip once with the ball, and female pitchers could cross their hip more, two or three times. Runners could not lead off any base until the ball passed the pitcher's hip, and only then could the runners attempt to steal the next base.

Fast-pitch appeared in the early '30s and was played from Steinbeck country in California, throughout the Texas oil fields, and up and down the East Coast. Some of the prominent players and teams include the ladies in *A League of Their Own*, Eddie Feigner with The King and His Court, and their female counterparts, The Queen and Her Maids. Those teams toured or barnstormed throughout the United States.

Fast-pitch softball started to wane in North Carolina in the early '50s. Military teams continued to play at unit and base levels until the early '80s. Today fast-pitch softball is predominately played by elementary, high school, and college girls or by men at the over-fifty world level. The men's version was replaced by slow-pitch softball.

Chapter 14

The Breakup

The federal tax wage laws brought about several national changes in 1938, including a higher minimum-wage salary, a minimum-age requirement, and the forty-hour workweek. These changes were welcomed by the workers, but it also meant that the rent to live in a mill house increased. Youngsters who were looking forward to working in the mills at twelve now had to wait until they were sixteen. It was believed that cotton mill tycoon Charlie Cannon had already established the eight-hour workday and forty-hour workweek before this law came into effect.

The most anticipated sports event of all times was scheduled to take place on June 23, 1938, at Yankee Stadium, New York, featuring the rematch between heavyweight fighters Joe Louis and Max Schmeling. Max Schmeling previously defeated Joe Louis in 1936 and since that time, had very favorable Nazi support, even though Schmeling never claimed to be a Nazi. At the time, the Nazis and Adolph Hitler were not considered to be a threat to the United States.

Most mill hillers wanted Joe Louis to win because the people in and around the mill hills were just as poor and could relate to the blacks who lived in Black Bottom or Silver Hill around Concord. Amazingly enough, even those prejudiced against blacks wanted Joe Louis to win because he was an American. This event was not just a fight between two heavyweights; it was symbolized as a battle between Nazi Germany, a dictatorship, and a free democracy.

On fight day, most radios were tuned in to hear the colossal battle that was about to take place. A small group of baseball players gathered around one radio set ready for the sporting event of the century. Heavy betting took place, not on who was going to win or lose, but in which round Joe Louis was supposed to knock Schmeling out.

As soon as the bout began, some of the ballplayers, including my father, started moving around the room like boxers in the ring, as if they were in the fight. Then the real Joe Louis unleashed a tirade of relentless punches on Max Schmeling so fast and furious to the point where everybody stood still, and in two minutes and four seconds of the first round, the fight was over. Those gathered around that radio started jumping around and celebrating with "I told you so, I knew he would do it."

Most listeners were in shock because very few had bet that Joe would win in the first round. Then Shad gave one of his quotes and said, "I told you that Joe Louis would beat the dog shit out of Max Schmeling," which is funny because there was no dog shit present. This was a Carolina phrase that meant not only did Schmeling lose, but he also got the hell beat out of him.

This victory placed Joe Louis above celebrity status. He became an American icon, an event that even topped Jessie Owens's accomplishments in the 1936 Summer Olympics. However, this battle between the titans was a prelude for what was about to happen.

Later that year, in October, the people in the area caught the tail end of a radio broadcast that startled everyone. They heard Orson Welles talk about martians invading different parts of the world. The people didn't know what to think. Some Carolinians started packing their things and were ready to flee the area, especially after they heard that the martians had landed in Virginia and were headed south.

One guy in the mill said, "They better not come down here, or they'll get what's coming to 'em."

The Carolinians and others were relieved when they found out that it was just a radio remake of H. G. Wells's *The War of the Worlds*. This was the first time anything like this was ever tried over the radio. This broadcast was tried again in another country, which had disastrous results.

It was difficult to determine when the marriage started to fray. Tension started to rise between Father and Ethel Marie after Ted was born. It didn't help that Pappy had a hell of a temper and was uncontrollable when he drank liquor. Even though Pappy didn't like how Grandpa Whittington treated his wife, the hell-raising knockdown drag-out lifestyle, coupled with the old adage or belief seemed to prevail, that some women were treated as property rather than as human beings

One morning they awoke, and one or both realized that either marriage or the person they had married was a big mistake. There were hints of infidelity; however, it will never be known which of the two perpetrated their vows and took that road of destruction. The truth will never be known because personal feelings were seldom, if ever, discussed by this generation, and the people who really knew have all passed away. Ethel Marie Whittington was a mystery that was never solved by the people who worked in the mill, her husband, or her two children.

The couple usually fought on the weekends on 69 Railroad Avenue, from the end of 1938 through 1940. Eventually, when the heat became too great, Ethel moved out of the house, left her husband and children and her home on Railroad Avenue, but continued to work at the Franklin. This left Shad with two young boys in the mill house. Shad had to have help with the boys. JM and Ted would stay with their uncle Will and aunt Nanny up in China Grove, North Carolina, or stay with their uncle Clarence up in Lincolnton.

During the next few years, Shad worked in the mill, played baseball, and tried to take care of the boys. Sometime during this separation, a custody battle ensued. It was a foregone conclusion that Ethel would win custody until Ethel's mother took the stand and testified against her daughter in the Cabarrus County courtroom. The judge ruled in Shad's favor, and Ethel Marie disappeared out of her son's lives. My brother Ted stated many years later he knew very little about his mom and did not know what became of her. All he heard were third-party stories, and the only thing he had from her was a picture of her standing in a field beside a bulldog. After a two-year separation, Judge Peyton McSwain granted the couple a divorce at the Cabarrus County Courthouse in Concord.

One day at work, before the divorce, Shad and another worker at Plant 9 got into a fight between two slubber frames. If either of them would have been knocked or pushed into the working slubbers, they could have easily been killed. Shad dropped the other guy with an uppercut to the stomach, in the aisle between the spinning slubber frames. The cause of the fight was Ethel Marie. This resulted in Cannon Mills's letting my father go, which meant he had to vacate his mill house. Now Shad was out of work, wifeless, with two young boys during the Depression, without a house, and was banned from playing baseball for Cannon Mills. If this wasn't bad enough, Adolph Hitler and the Nazi party started upsetting the whole Apple Cart in Europe. Some Carolinians described it as "Hitler started showing his ass."

Chapter 15

Hitler's Move for World Power

American attitude was to stay out of any foreign entanglements and not repeat the mistakes that led to WW1. The people had spoken through the Pathe News Polls and were dead set against being dragged into another world war. Little did most Americans know that Germany had a plan and had been executing that plan at an accelerated rate. When most European countries were still reeling from the effects of the Great Depression, hardly anyone noticed the rapid progression that was taking place in Germany.

Adolph Hitler became chancellor of Germany in 1933, and soon after President Hindenburg died, there wasn't any opposition to his rise for power and glory. Hitler promised the people work and bread, very important aspects with 33 percent of the people out of work. He was an anti-communist and an anti-Semite, which was in vogue in Germany at the time. Someone or some group had to be the scapegoat for the German defeat in WW1.

In 1935, Hitler ordered conscription, drafted able-bodied soldiers and pilots into the Wehrmacht and Luftwaffe. He put the German people to work building military vehicles and aircraft. By 1936, he linked up with his bald-headed goose-stepping buddy

Mussolini to support Franco's drive for power in Spain. During the same year, Germany hosted the Summer Olympics in Berlin and reoccupied the Rhineland. Now this was a man who as Pappy would say, "Had the world by the ass."

After Hitler unveiled his military might to visiting dignitaries from around the world, he stepped in and annexed Austria on March 12, 1938. By October 1938, he convinced France and England to give him the Sudetenland, the northern and western border regions of Czechoslovakia. There was very little France and England could do because their countries were suffering from the Depression and were fearful of another world war.

When Hitler and his cronies realized this weakness, by March 1939, he ordered German troops to march in and occupy the rest of Czechoslovakia. Amazingly enough, all this land grab was done without a shot being fired.

Things were a little different for Germany's next move. The last week of August 1939, Germany signed a nonaggression pact with Russia, called the Molotov-Ribbentrop Pact, so Poland was divided even before German troops crossed the Polish border to invade on September 1, 1939.

On September 3, England and France declared war on Germany, and radios all over the world announced in various indigenous languages that World War 2 had just begun. This worried the people on the Franklin Mill Hill, especially those who fought in WW1. While Pappy was celebrating his twenty-fifth birthday, everyone became very solemn when the radio announcer stated that Warsaw had fallen, and on October 6, 1939, the whole ball game was over for Poland.

This was just a warm-up for what would happen next. Norway was invaded in April 1940, and on May 10, Hitler began a bold move by invading Holland, Belgium, and France simultaneously. The people on the Franklin Mill Hill and the rest of the world could not believe it when Dunkirk fell on June 4, 1940.

Pap told me many years later that "Germany moved through France like shit through a goose." Now even the mill workers in North Carolina knew that a threat loomed on the other side of the Atlantic, poised on the shores of France. Oceans could be crossed easily and were no longer considered to be the protective moats surrounding the castle. The battle for France was over, and the battle for Britain was about to begin.

Millions of American and Canadian listeners heard suspenseful radio broadcasts coming in live from London as the Luftwaffe bombed the hell out of England. North Carolinian listeners knew this radio personality all too well because the announcer, Edward R. Murrow, was born and raised right up the road from Concord, in Guilford County, near Greensboro. Unlike the previous Orson Welles broadcasts, this was the war of this world happening in real time.

In 1940, America was still neutral, and because the growing concern of the situation in Europe, American leaders decided to increase military strength. This was the first time national conscription was ordered during a time of peace, requiring the registration of all men between the ages of twenty-one and forty-five. This was a national lottery-type drawing. The Secretary of War, Henry L. Stimson, drew the first number out of a large jar, presented the number to President Roosevelt, in which the president announced number 158.

The USS *North Carolina* (BB 55) was launched on June 13, 1940. At the time, she was the deadliest sea weapon on the planet. This femme fatal was bad and beautiful. Her twin sister was the USS *Washington*. On July 19, the Two-Ocean Navy Act was signed into law by President Roosevelt. The Tri-Partite Act or the Berlin Treaty was signed by Germany, Italy, and Japan on Pap's twenty-sixth birthday, September 27, 1940.

Meanwhile, the people back in Cabarrus County were ready to watch the start of the 1940 Carolina Textile Baseball season. The scheduled Saturday morning baseball game between Cabarrus and Brown mills was about to start. Shad Whittington was catching for Brown Mill, and a thirteen- year-old Bill Ford showed up to watch the game. Bill Ford's nickname was Duck because his daddy said that when he walked, he waddled like a duck.

Pappy knew that baseballs cost a lot of money and said, "Ducky, if you get on top the outfield wall, and if somebody hits one out of the park, you can get to the ball first, That ball will be yours."

Bill Ford said, "Shad Rack hit three home runs that game. His last home run almost knocked me off the wooden center field wall."

Chapter 16

Shad Meets Ted Williams

Things were looking pretty bad for the Franklin Mill Hiller who just got banned from the community, which had been his home for a quarter of a century, but when you can play ball and run slubbers like Shad could, there were other mills that would take you in a heartbeat. That happened to be Brown Mill.

Even though cars were becoming more plentiful, very few mill hillers owned or drove cars, so it was quite common to see Shad, JM, and Ted walking to and from evening and weekend baseball games together. They ate many meals together at the Brown Mill Cafe. Very little is known if there were any female prospects who were willing to step in and assume the role of lover and wife.

Pap viewed women as pariahs or Jezebels of some sort, quite normal for those who have suffered from a terrible relationship or a nasty divorce because injured parties tend to stereotype or condemn the other gender to hell. There is no telling how many one-night stands, trysts, or transient women tried to fill this void, but many years passed before a serious attempt was made for Pappy to look for, much less find, a woman who could fill that emotional gap.

The baseball scene was going as strong as ever; the mill teams were at their height from 1938 through 1941. Vernon Ford and Bill Hooks made their baseball debut in the textile league during the 1939 season. Bill Hooks, a power-hitting third baseman and shortstop, had an arm like a high-powered rifle.

When Bill was only sixteen years old, during the 1940 season, he was playing class D baseball in the Florida East Coast League. Vernon, the plus-two-hundred pound, six-foot-four, Cabarrus Mill center fielder, was a low-ball hitter who could hit home runs so far, it was unbelievable. An entire book could be dedicated to capture the exploits of Vernon Harold Ford.

Pappy played baseball with Fred Parnell from the Norcott Mill area. Fred was a left-handed hitter who played for Norcott Mill as early as 1930. He had three sons: Bryant; Fred, a right-hander; and Jack, originally played center field but later became a pitcher and a Kannapolis policeman.

Bryant Jr. told me that my father and his grandfather, being left-handed hitters, hated to bat against left-handed pitchers, especially if they were wild. It just so happened that they were batting against a wild left-hander that day. Pappy and Fred batted third and fourth in the lineup and had running bets with each other as to who would get the most hits off this wild man on the mound. It happened to be two outs when Pappy came up to bat, and right away, the pitcher stuck a fast ball right into Pappy's ribs, so he was awarded first base.

Pap led off as if he was going to steal second, but the left-handed pitcher had a smooth move to first base. Fred, now batting at the time, already had two strikes against him when the pitcher threw the ball to first and the first baseman tagged my father out. At the same time, Fred swung at what he thought was a pitch coming to the plate. Immediately, the base umpire called Pappy out, and the plate umpire called Fred out, which ended up as a double play, with four outs in one inning on the same pitch. Everyone who saw this had a conniption fit. When Pap told his version of the story, the left-handed pitcher was also cross-eyed.

If the textile mills were the body of the area, then playing baseball was the soul. By this time, if an able-bodied man didn't play baseball, he probably would have been labeled as an infidel or a communist.

Pappy also played for and against the hard-throwing, hard-hitting, left-handed pitcher, George Hatley, whom he called Big George. Pappy, also at a corner store, called Gene's Short Stop, owned by Gene Verble, a retired Major League baseball player. It was previously known as Jackson Park Grill.

The Jackson Park Grill was located inside the Y intersection of the old Charlotte Highway and Wilshire Drive, one of the spots where the ballplayers met and told stories. Gene Verble told me, "One day your daddy showed up at the store, and we were looking at a rifle that someone was showing off." Gene asked, "Shad what do you think of this rifle?"

Pap said, "It looks pretty good."

Then a bird flew up on the water tower, which was quite a long way off, and Gene asked, "Do you think you could hit that bird with this rifle?"

And Shad said, "Yes."

No one there believed it could be done. Then Shad took the rifle, loaded it, put it up to his shoulder, and shot the bird off the tower, then he handed the rifle back to the man and never said another word. Gene told me, "Your daddy could shoot a rifle better than anybody he had ever seen."

Although Pap didn't live on the Franklin hill anymore, he still kept in touch and stayed close to those he grew up with and would stop at the Short Street Grocery but spent more time at Dabbs & Eisenhower Grocery at the corner of Robinson and Main. Mr. C.W. Dabbs was the second-shift card room overseer, and Mr. Eisenhower ran drawing machines for the Franklin.

Pappy would visit with a thirteen-year-old Duck Ford working at Dabbs Grocery and have talks with him from time to time. Both grocery stores would take customer orders and deliver those goods in advance to the workers' homes. A tab would be maintained, and the workers would come by the store to pay their bill after they received their checks. Mr. Ford said, "A loaf of bread only cost 9¢ at the time."

Pap and Vernon Ford, Duck's elder cousin, started to become friends, and by this time, Vernon had been working at the spinning-department in Franklin for over a year. Vernon had more nicknames than any of the other ballplayers. Some called him the Big V; his family members called him Pinto; Pappy called him Toad; Howard Hooks called him Uncle Vernon, although not related; and the children called him Bubby.

There were so many leagues in North Carolina: the local textile league, Sally League (South-Atlantic Association), Granite-Belt League, Piedmont League, Yadkin Valley League, Coastal Plains League, Tri-State and NC State Leagues. It was hard to follow.

One of Brother Ted's earlier memories included the time he was sitting in the grandstands at the Brown Mill Ballpark watching Pappy play. Ted said the fans filled the bleachers and were packed along both foul lines on each side of the field. Most men wore fedoras at the time. The crowd was so thick; if anyone hit a line drive into the crowd, they would not have time to get out of the way.

Pap came up to the plate and hit a home run way out of the ballpark. As soon as Pap went into his home run trot, the people along the first base line ran over and started stuffing $1 and $5 bills in his uniform jersey. The crowd along the third base line did the same as Father headed toward home plate. He made more money from that single home run than he would make working an entire month in the mill, something equivalent to today's rock star status. In all my years of playing ball, I have never witnessed anything like what Ted described.

Most everybody around Concord knew about the upcoming ball game that was scheduled to be played in Statesville between the Cincinnati Reds and the Boston Red Sox. Many club managers would schedule warm-up or pick-up games between their regular schedules en route to other cities.

The Statesville ballpark was filled with a lot of Carolina League players that carpooled over to see the game. Most fans wanted to see Ted Williams, who was tearing the cover off the ball that year. Shad saw the game and got to talk to Ted Williams after the game.

Pap had heard that Ted Williams was stuck-up and conceited, but those two hitters met and talked like they had known each other for most of their lives. They had a lot in common; both were left-handed hitters, both threw right-handed, and both players spent many hours trying to perfect their craft. They were hitting divas that spent most of their time outdoors; they loved to hunt and fish. Each had exceptional eyesight; Shad had 20/10 vision at the time.

Later that year, on September 27, 1941, Pappy's twenty-seventh birthday, Ted Williams ended the season with a 406 batting average. Pappy always spoke highly of Ted Williams, and many believe that Williams was the best hitter that baseball has or will ever see. His 406 season batting average has never been broken.

The War Klaxon Sounds

The movie *Sergeant York* opened in theaters on July 2, 1941, and was an instant box-office hit. Later that year, Congress stepped in and pulled the movie from the theaters, labeling the movie as a propaganda film intended to incite a nation to go to war. America was teetering between intervention and isolation. There were three hundred German bunds or clubs scattered throughout the United States, and many could care less what Hitler or Mussolini did in Europe. People started to accept the speeches Charles Lindberg was making about a Hitler-dominated Europe.

Then the unspeakable happened that shook the world; radios and newspapers across the nation reported that the Japanese had bombed Pearl Harbor. Most people in Carolina asked, "Where in hell is Pearl Harbor?"

Americans became enraged because of the way Japan sneaked up on America without making an announcement of war.

On December 8, Pres. Franklin D. Roosevelt made his "Day of Infamy" speech, one of the most powerful speeches ever given. America listened intently as Roosevelt declared war on the Empire of Japan. If you were to hear this speech in its entirety, I am sure you would be impressed. Every time I hear this speech, it fills me with a mix of sadness and pride, but could you imagine how it sounded when Americans heard the speech for the first time?

Three days later, Adolph Hitler declared war on the United States, and the German generals realized their leader had just declared war on the most industrialized nation on the planet. Most Germans remembered that it was the United States that tipped the scales to ensure German defeat during WW1.

The Tri-Partite Act called for Germany, Italy, or Japan to come to the others' aid in case any of the three countries were attacked. However, Japan was not attacked; Japan was the aggressor. Had Hitler not declared war on America, the United States might have only been involved fighting in the Pacific, leaving the French and British Commonwealth Nations to battle Italy and Germany. Hitler's declaration of war freed Roosevelt, and America's European isolationism came to a swift end.

The same day President Roosevelt made his speech, Bob Feller, the best pitcher in baseball, joined the military, and eight people from the Franklin Mill joined the navy. Americans no longer worried if *Sergeant York* was a war film and didn't care much about what Lindberg had to say. By this time, Jim Whittington was a grown man, and as stated in a previous chapter, he grew with the country. The United States, like Pappy, was as mature as they had ever been.

The Carolina scene changed at a rapid pace. Men were signing up for military service; industries started tooling up to produce military goods instead of the old items of peace. Cannon Mills produced materials for making uniforms, and mills started running three shifts seven days a week.

After war was declared, the draft went into full swing, quite different from the lottery-type drawing known prior to the war. Induction centers were filled beyond capacity-many volunteers had to be turned away and were told to come back at a later date.

Thousands of volunteers, dressed in all sorts of attire, from suits to bib overalls, stood in lines. Inductees were classified as 1A, single and ready to go; 1S, single but in school; 3A, married or with dependents; and 4F, which usually meant that person failed the medical exam. There were exceptions and other considerations; for example, if a single man was 1S and enrolled in school, he would not be called to service until the high school or college term was finished.

Those not in school were sent immediately to their respective training centers and branches of service. Those married members, 3A, were to leave at a later date, given some time to get family matters in order. Those 4F members who were classified as underweight were told to eat a lot of bananas, drink a lot of water, then come back to see if they could make minimum weight.

Those volunteers who weren't old enough were told that they had to have written permission from their parents to join; some just flat out lied about their age. Other 4F members were just unsuitable for military service.

Some farmers were exempted from the draft because people had to eat, and the nation not only had to consider filling and staffing an army, army air corps, navy, and marine corps, but there was also concern about back-filling positions in an American industry those volunteers vacated when they joined the military.

This is when American women stepped up to the plate and saved the day. They changed the face of the Work Progress Administration (WPA), where previously, only the breadwinner was supposed to be awarded a job. Now that home-front breadwinner was the wife.

America was way behind the power curve and had to catch up with Germany, Italy, and Japan who had been preparing for war years in advance. The nation was like a slow-moving dynamo trying to overcome inertia; those wheels and gears started turning at a slow pace but soon started churning out the greatest war machine the world had ever seen.

Japanese Admiral Yamamoto stated that Japan had just awakened a sleeping giant. Now that giant was awake, rising from its slumber and ready to kick some ass.

North Carolina became a military encampment and boasted to have more servicemen within its boundaries than any other state. Fort Bragg's ranks swelled to sixty-seven thousand; there was a large coast guard base at Elizabeth City, an aircraft/glider base at

Laurinburg/Maxton, two marine bases, Cherry Point and Camp Lejeune.

Aerial gunnery was practiced at Camp Holly, while female pilots flew planes overhead, towing targets, enabling novice gunners practice to improve their shooting skills. Wilmington contained a vast shipbuilding yard that eventually employed twenty thousand workers of all races, colors, and creeds. Ships started slipping into the Cape Fear River at an alarming rate. GCT-10 became a large induction center in Greensboro for those to be sent overseas. The military was still segregated at the time, and there were training camps established for the African American soldiers, sailors and marines as well.

Despite this, Germany didn't waste any time. U-boats started sinking American ships from New York Harbor all the way to the Gulf of Mexico. Carolina residents could hear the explosions just off Wrightsville Beach, and throngs of people watched our tankers burn offshore. The point off Cape Lookout of the outer banks became known as Torpedo Alley. Residents living near the shores of the outer banks could feel their windows shake when German torpedoes found their mark. Many residents spent sleepless nights worrying whether they would be invaded, captured, or killed.

Those U-boats had a field day because the lights on shore silhouetted those targeted ships. This mistake was corrected when the coast guard started patrolling Carolina beaches and enforcing mandatory blackouts. Later in the war, Plant 1 in Kannapolis was even blacked out at night because of fear of inland bombing.

Commodities and resources had to be diverted toward the war effort, so a rationing system was established. Ration books were issued by the county. Sugar, gas, and women's nylons became very dear. There were scrap metal and aluminum drives needed to build aircraft, and vast amounts of rubber was required for aircraft and transport vehicles.

The people in and around Cabarrus County were encouraged to walk, take the bus, or carpool to save gas. The word was if anyone saw a person driving alone, whoever saw them would say, "Look at that man or that hussy driving around with Hitler."

No one wanted to be accused of driving with Hitler.

There were so many volunteers who joined or were drafted; the NC State, Class D, Baseball League had to be discontinued. Local baseball was such an integral part of home life; NC State League was reinstated and renamed Victory League. This league comprised of ballplayers who were awaiting orders; some classified as 4F, while others were exempt from military service. Many gaps existed in old State League lineups; now Victory League was filled with high school or college baseball players, namely Bill Ford and Gene Verble.

Chapter 18

From the Mountains to the Sea

Clarence Lee Whittington, Pappy's oldest brother, was a quiet simple man with legendary power and strength. He was tougher than an old cedar tree. Clarence stood about six-foot-six and weighed about the same as most of the adult black bears that roamed freely around the western part of the state. He was pure muscle and brawn and usually dressed in old overalls topped with a big floppy brimmed straw hat. He spoke in a loud and booming voice and would scare most people when he said hello.

Those who knew him called him Dynamite. He stayed in the hills so much, he felt out of place when he visited a local town or was near a large gathering of people. He was a modern-day mountain man and was truly a mountain of a man.

Yet despite this, he did not flaunt his strength or come across as a hard case. He had a kind heart and projected a good general attitude toward others. He never drank a drop of beer or whisky, but the local moonshiners kept a wide berth from Clarence Whittington.

After Clarence left the Whittington home on Robinson Street in 1920, he fell in with a rough crowd. Uncle Clarence got crossways with the local ruffian considered to be unbeatable. During their short conflict, Clarence hit the man once and left his opponent lying unconscious underneath a T-Model Ford. The guy had to be helped out from under the car by several of his buddies, but the blow messed the man up for the rest of his life. An arrest followed, and Clarence ended up doing hard time in the local pen.

After Clarence served his time, he could be seen working at the local feed store and would commonly carry four brown burlap oat sacks by the ears or the corners of the feed sacks, two in each hand. Each sack weighed about one hundred pounds. He would toss the sacks into the bed of a wagon as if they were pillows. During one loading session, the impact of those bags slamming into the bed of the wagon spooked the mules, and the wagon owner cried out, "Damn, Dynamite, you're scaring my mules and tearing up my wagon!"

The feed store owner added, "Dynamite is the strongest man he had ever seen."

Pappy remembered helping his brother change tires on the old car by sticking pine logs underneath the car's axle while Clarence lifted the front end of the car off the ground. After the tire was changed, he would lift the car up again, and Pap would remove the log. Uncle Clarence didn't need a jack.

After leaving Concord, Clarence ventured toward the western part of the state, near what Father called the Brushy Mountains, the foothills of the Appalachians. He met and married a Cherokee woman named Beulah Mae Christopher and settled down in a three-room house on rural Route 5. Clarence share-cropped that land and worked the cattle and mules for years until the owner deeded him the property.

Clarence was very competitive; after all, he was a Whittington. He loved to pitch horseshoes and could shot pool very well. Pitching horseshoes was a Whittington ritual and was the main mode of competition among family. Whenever Pappy beat his elder brother in a horseshoe game, Clarence would switch to the smaller mule shoes and claim home team advantage.

Clarence loved to shoot pool at one of the bars near his property around Lincolnton. During one pool game, Clarence was winning money, hand over fist. Suddenly, the guy he was shooting against lost his temper and hit Clarence. Clarence grabbed the man by the sides with both hands, dug his fingers deep into the man's flesh. The man started screaming in pain. Clarence picked him up, carried him over to the wall, and hung him by his overalls on a metal hat rack, like someone would hang up a coat.

Clarence left the pool room and left the man hanging on the metal peg, and the guys in the pool room laughed at the man to scorn. The embarrassed pool shooter never spoke to Clarence ever again and would cross over to the other side of the street when he saw Clarence coming down the road.

Brother Ted recalled one particular visit to Clarence's place. Clarence looked down at Ted and asked in his booming voice, "Boy, do you want some fried chicken?"

Ted answered, "Yes, Uncle Clarence."

Clarence had a lot of chickens roaming around in the yard, and all of a sudden, Clarence reached down, grabbed a rooster, wrung the chicken's neck, and snapped the chicken's head off in a flash. The chicken started flopping and flapping around, and Ted thought the roster was attacking him and started climbing the picket fence to get away. Brother Ted said, "Even today, when I have fried chicken, I think about that and start laughing."

JM and Ted really enjoyed spending time with their uncle because he took them everywhere and would show them how to do chores on the farm. He let them be boys but told them to mind themselves around the mules. This world was much different from what the boys experienced growing up on the Franklin Mill Hill, but they loved every minute of it.

Many of Shad's buddies joined the service, which included George Hatley, Willard and Marvin Mauney, Bill and Howard Hooks, as well as Johnson Strube. Shad's situation was quite different because he was divorced, the sole provider for two boys, which legally made him exempt from the draft. It is uncertain if he knew this fact or whether the call for duty and patriotic fervor was the overriding factor in his decision to join. Maybe he felt he could provide for his dependents better with a military paycheck.

Willard Mauney had been playing baseball for the Concord Weavers since 1939 and could cover the outfield like a cheetah. Those spectators all agreed that Willard could play left field better than most had ever seen. The fans recalled, at the crack of the bat, seeing Willard turning and running full sprint, climbing the bank in left field like a mountain goat, and at the last second, turn and catch the ball. That catch was immediately followed by a perfect throw to second base. But what made this feat almost impossible: Willard made that throw while standing on a bank with a thirty-degree slant.

Willard was also a left-handed hitter with an excellent snap cut. He could drag bunt better than most people could lay down a sacrifice bunt. If his infield hit or bunt hit the ground more than twice, he would be safely standing on first base. Stealing second was almost a foregone conclusion. There was a vast amount of baseball improvement and physical maturity since Willard and Pappy chased foul balls along Three Mile Branch on the edge of this same ball field years earlier.

Willard's younger brother, Richard, turned down for military service because of the loss of or the lack of sight in one of his eyes, earned him the nickname "Bad-Eyed Mauney." Two stories exist as to how Richard's eye was injured. One story came from one of Richard's nephews. Richard was hand fishing for catfish, called graveling, one day, and as he pulled a big blue channel catfish out from among the rocks, the fish spiked him in the eye. Pappy's version was quite different. Pap stated that Richard was injured while rabbit-hunting with his brothers. After a rabbit was flushed out of the brush, one of the hunters took a shot at the rabbit. The shot hit the dirt, skipped up, and hit Richard in the side of the face. Regardless of which story is true, this left Richard Mauney with questionable, if any, sight available in one eye. This may have stopped Richard from joining the military but did not keep him from playing baseball. Richard stayed back and played baseball in Victory League.

Marvin Mauney joined the army, and Bill Hooks, who had been playing professional baseball in Florida, joined the navy shortly after December 1941, one of the earliest from the Franklin Mill Hill group to join. His younger brother, Howard, would end up serving in the army at the tail end of WW2. Johnston Strube, a wild right-handed pitcher, also joined the army. Vernon Ford, declined from military service for physical reasons, stayed home, worked in the spinning department at the Franklin, and played baseball in the textile league.

It was decided that brother Willie would care for JM and Ted, and Shad would send money home to support the boys. Will and Nanny never had children, and at the time Will was overseeing a farm at the Old Fink Place in China Grove, North Carolina. Now that the boys would be taken care of, Shad joined the navy.

Father was met by his mother, brother Will, Nanny, JM, and Ted at the train depot in Concord. Ted was holding on to his grandmother's leg, wondering when he would see his Pappy again. It was quite a tearful departure before he boarded that train, the first of several passenger trains that would eventually take him to Great Lakes, Illinois, for naval basic seamanship.

After Shad was comfortably seated and the train rolled out of the station and the pain in his heart waned a bit, he thought about the first train ride he took in 1931 and started laughing. The situation was altogether different for this train ride because he was embarking on a journey that would eventually take him all over the world, and those upcoming vistas would make the world he was leaving behind seem quite small. This was the first time he would be away from everything he knew.

This scene was being played out all across the United States. Millions of American boys and women were doing whatever they could to help the cause. The recruits came from all walks of life; many had never fired a gun, ridden in a boat, been off the ground, or had even seen the ocean. Those Americans had one goal in mind: to grind the Empire of Japan, Hitler's Germany, and Mussolini's Italian forces into the dirt, blast them from the face of the earth, and wipe out everything they stood for.

Great Lakes, Illinois, proved to be the coldest spot on earth Seaman Whittington had experienced so far. The sailors took target-practice, learned to shoot a .22-caliber Model 75 Winchester bolt-action rifle to save on ammunition cost. The navy stayed with the Springfield Model 1903, 30-06 rifle, instead upgrading to the M1 Garand. Pappy didn't have any problems with marksmanship;

he was the second-best shot in his outfit, only bested by another trainee from Tennessee. He participated in daily calisthenics, received medical attention that he could not previously afford, performed close-order drills and the manual of arms with his Springfield rifle.

Before Shad left North Carolina, the radio stations were not only playing country, gospel, and hillbilly music, but also had ushered in the big band era. Tunes like Artie Shaw's "Begin the Beguine," Glenn Miller's "In the Mood," Les Brown's Band of Renown, Bennie Goodman, and Tommy Dorsey hits were being played as well. One could not listen to a radio station for more than an hour without hearing a Bing Crosby tune. The sailors looked forward to their liberty and danced all night to these tunes. I have heard it said, "Had it not been for Douglas MacArthur and Glenn Miller, the United States might have lost the war."

While training at Great Lakes, Seaman Whittington received a couple of letters from his son James (JM) Whittington Jr., informing him that the situation was not so good for the boys back in China Grove. Shad worried about how his brother would care for the boys and had arranged for friends to check on his sons' progress from time to time. Those friends confirmed that the money sent home for their support was not making it to the boys but was spent for other purposes.

Shad consulted his chain of command and through their advice, arranged for the boys to be transferred to a state-approved orphanage home.

Brother Ted tells the story from a four- or five-year-old perspective. He said, "JM and I were at the Old Fink Place when two people drove up in what looked like a hearse. Then a woman dressed in a black dress, wearing a black veil, got out of the car, walked over to Will, talked to him a short while, showed him some papers, then took me and my brother by the hand and put us in the car. It was a long trip, which took most of the day, over dusty roads. I fell asleep, and when I woke up, we had arrived at the Cypes Orphanage Home, near Lincolnton, North Carolina."

The document shown to Uncle Will was custody authority, a Western Union telegram sent from Shad Whittington.

After basic, Seaman Whittington was assigned to a destroyer. The destroyers were known as the Greyhounds of the fleet, but sailors called them tin cans. The destroyer provided convoy antisubmarine and antiaircraft protection. Shad was assigned to many different gun crew and became one with the various weapons that were aboard. This included the five-inch, 38s, the three-inch .50s, 40 mm pom-poms, .50-caliber machine guns, and the Y-guns that propelled the ash cans (depth charges) out laterally from the ship to sink submarines. He was pretty good at shooting things and hitting the target, so he felt right at home with all that fire power.

Initially, the new recruits didn't jell; the ones from the North or larger metropolitan areas made fun of the rural, Southern country-bumpkin types, like Father. After Shad busted a couple of them in the mouth or backhanded one or two in the shower, they started to keep their comments to themselves. Shad told one, "You are supposed to be so smart. This is not about where we are from, it is about where we are going, you nitwit."

Shad learned this team concept from playing baseball in the Carolina Textile League. As soon as those city-dwellers found out how well those country boys could shoot, their attitude changed significantly. They began to seek help from those illiterate, uneducated, backwoods-raised sorts, to improve their own shooting skills. Soon those differences didn't matter anymore, and their comments were, "Man, when the guns start blazing, I want those Southern boys by my side."

Aboard ship, Shad linked up with two of his compadres, Paul Azark from Arkansas and Watts from Mississippi. This was not irregular for a Carolinian to bond with other Southerners; a very useful combination because Paul Azark was a wrestler, Pappy boxed, and Watts was a tall and powerful swimmer. Pap always referred to his buddy from Mississippi as Watts, he never used his full name, so I never knew if Watts was his first or his last name. Pappy said, "Watts could outswim Buster Crabbe."

They were hell-raisers, and it was a good thing to know that your running buddies could take care of each other, if there was a brawl. During Pap's time, knockdown drag-out fights were just another way of expressing oneself and was viewed quite differently than it is today. After most fights, the opponents would shake hands and continue on as if nothing had happened. Fighting was just a physical form of communication.

This was evident after Shad stopped into port at Southampton, England, for shore duty. The sailors were quite taken by the English hospitality shown for the Americans by British soldiers and sailors at this large and elegant port bar. It was a pleasure to know that the English Allies were quite proud that America finally threw in with the British to defeat a common enemy.

As the night progressed, rounds of drinks were bought and shared between the Yanks and the Brits. After each round of drinks was served, toasts and short speeches were given at each table. Everything was fine until after one American sailor bought his third round, a British soldier raised his glass, and proclaimed, "God bless the Yanks, and God save the Queen."

This irritated the sailor, and the sailor calmly said to the soldier, "Look here, I appreciate the fact that we are allies in this war, sharing drinks between fighting men, but these drinks are for us, and you can go fuck that queen."

Immediately, a gigantic fight broke out that involved everyone in that Southampton bar. They tore the bar all to hell. The local police and the shore patrol was needed to break up the melee. The next morning the captain had thirty-five sailors standing at attention along the port rail of Pappy's vessel.

The skipper said that they had caused $3,500 worth of damage and put many British Allies in the hospital. The old man chewed them out, docked their pay, and restricted them to the ship. Whittington, Azark, and Watts were right in the middle of this rowdy group.

One night, while Seaman Whittington was standing guard duty or watch, he was told to deliver an urgent message to the old man without delay. Sentries weren't supposed to read messages. When Dad closed the bulkhead door and the red light illuminated, he read this hot message. The message, typed out in capital letters, read, "26 GERMAN DIVE BOMBERS SPOTTED 30 MILES TO THE EAST, HEADING WESTBOUND. POSSIBLE TARGET, THE CONVOY."

After Pappy read this message, his legs grew wobbly, and he leaned up against the bulkhead for a few seconds then continued his trek toward the old man's quarters. After reporting to the captain with "Urgent message, sir," the captain read the message and looked into Seaman Whittington's eyes and asked, "Did you read this message, sailor?"

Pap answered, "Yes, sir,"

The skipper added, "Sailor, you know this is a punishable offense, but due to the circumstances, I will overlook this situation. Now take the ladder down to your quarters, put on your battle gear, and don't mention a word about this to anyone."

Before Seaman Whittington made it to his bunk, the ship's alarm sounded with the announcement to prepare for battle stations. His tin can was about to experience its first baptism by fire.

There were many front-porch swing sessions that took place over many years as Pappy told us about his adventures in the navy. One adventure involved a training session where the gun crew had to take apart, clean, and reassemble .50-caliber machine guns. Watts, Azark, and Whittington decided to skip this training because they had done this before and wanted to enjoy their onshore pass a little longer.

The very next day all the .50-caliber weapons and gun crew were standing by their weapons, ready for inspection. The chief petty officer barked, "Tear down those weapons!"

All the crew responded in kind, including the Whittington-Azark-Watts crew, with military precision. Then the petty officer and the old man walked down the line, and after seeing that all the crew had disassembled their weapons, the petty officer shouted, "Reassemble your weapons!" Only this time the Whittington gun crew had reassembled their weapon and had a few pieces left over.

Seaman Whittington assured his crew not to worry and instructed Watts to hide the leftover pieces under a piece of canvas that was nearby. The inspection team walked back up the line, and everything seemed to be satisfactory. Whittington told his crew, "I told you we would be all right."

Then an ammo team started dropping off belts of ammunition alongside each weapon. It was at this point that Dad's crew started to worry. The petty officer commanded, "Load your weapons."

Everyone did so in like fashion, then the petty officer and the old man went down the line again and stopped by each weapon and gave the order, "Number 1 weapon, fire, Number 2," each in turn, and they eventually made to Whittington's crew, and their weapon fired just like all the previous guns.

Just before the inspection team could progress to the next weapon in line, Watts blurted out, "Sir, wait a minute," then pulled out the hidden pieces under the canvas and added, "Sir, here are three pieces of this gun you don't need."

Consequently, Whittington, Azark, and Watts were assigned additional punishment duties.

I can remember Pappy sitting out on the front-porch swing, staring off into the horizon, reminiscing about those times he served in the navy. It seemed that he would be thousands of miles away, then somehow he would come back to us and tell whoever was on the porch, "There were times when I saw the Pacific when it was as smooth as skim-sweet milk, not a ripple in sight. Then a few days later, gale force winds blew up swells that looked as high as the Brushy Mountains," then added, "that was the only time I ever got seasick."

S. S. Carole Lombard Launched

With Captain Clark Gable, husband of the late actress, Carole Lombard, and other movie notables in attendance, the 10,500-ton Liberty ship, S. S. Carole Lombard slides down the ways in launching ceremonies at the California Shipbuilding Corp. in Wilmington, Calif.

Chapter 19

Jane Alice Peters and the Liberty Ship

It seems uncanny that Jane Alice Peters, born in Fort Wayne, Indiana, in 1908, would have any connection with a Carolina boy, Shad Whittington, born in 1914. Although the two never met, this is how one's legacy and the other's destiny crossed paths.

Jane Alice Peters went to Hollywood and became known as the actress Carole Lombard. She met Clark Gable in 1937, the hottest star in the business at the time, and they married in 1939. To tell you how big the war effort became, Alan Ladd, Tyrone Power, Jimmy Stewart, Glenn Ford, and Frank Capra, just to name a few, joined. Frank Capra began making the *Why We Fight* series. The Hollywood crowd was not exempt from the war.

Bob Hope, Bing Crosby, and Carole Lombard all participated in massive w-bond drives. In 1942, Carole, returning from a record-breaking home-state war-bond drive and en route to her home in California, had just landed in Las Vegas, Nevada, to refuel. After refueling the Transcontinental and Western Air DC-3, the plane took off with Carole, her mother, Clark Gable's press agent, fifteen army servicemen and the plane's crew on board.

Just twenty-three minutes after takeoff, the plane crashed into Double Up Peak, and all on board were killed. Carole had always urged her husband to join, and shortly after her death, Clark joined the army air corps and made war films about the Eighth Air Force based out of England. It has been said that Clark Gable never fully recovered after losing Carole Lombard.

America started turning out many not-so-attractive cargo ships as fast as could be made. President Roosevelt said they were dreadful-looking objects. *Time* magazine called them ugly ducklings. The cargo ship's designation was EC2-S-C1. EC stood for emergency cargo, the 2 meant that the ship was between 400 and 450 feet long, and the S meant the ship was steam-engine-driven. These vessels were the answer to Lend-Lease that provided war supplies to the ports of England, Murmansk, Russia, and other places around the globe.

Despite this bad press and ugly appearance, on September 27, 1941, the same day Shad turned twenty-seven years old and Ted Williams batted 406, President Roosevelt launched the SS *Patrick Henry* and cited a portion of Patrick Henry's speech: "Give me liberty, or give me death."

This ceremony marked a great launching of ships to support England's freedom, and from that day forward, those ugly ducklings were called Liberty Ships. From 1941 through 1945, America launched 2,710 Liberty Ships, the largest number of ships ever produced of a single design.

These were merchant marine vessels, hence the SS designation instead of USS, and was commanded by a merchant marine captain and crew. Those ships were augmented by regular United States Navy personnel, assigned to man the guns and perform assigned ship duties.

Many of those Liberty Ships were named after any organization or individuals that had raised $2 million in war-bond drives. It just so happened that a ship designated as number 2557 was named after Carole Lombard. The ship was launched from a California port by Irene Dunne and Capt. Clark Gable on January 15, 1944, ten years to the day before I was born. Amazingly enough, by the time the

Carole Lombard was launched, WW2 had swallowed up the Great Depression.

Seamen Whittington, Azark, and Watts were in the fleet, and they heard about this Liberty Ship duty and volunteered to augment the merchant marines. They were told how much better the duty was, more liberty, better food, and they would be able see foreign ports all over the world, which happened to be right up their alley. Reasons like this was why they volunteered for Liberty Ship duty.

By a stroke of luck or by divine intervention, those three sailors got their wish and found themselves standing along with the other USN sailors on the deck of the SS *Carole Lombard*, ready to receive their in-brief. The assigned briefer began with, "Men, I welcome you aboard the SS *Carole Lombard*, and as you men know, she was a fine lady. Things you have heard about Liberty Ship duty is definitely true, and the merchant marines hope that the gun crew can help protect all on board.

"I must add that this vessel is commanded by a merchant marine captain that has the same authority that any other regular navy commander and will not tolerate slackness or breaches of duty. But, men what they didn't tell you about this glorious assignment is that we will be carrying precious goods and war materials that our enemy wants to stop us from delivering to our allies. The Liberty Ships are their primary target above all others. Most of the time we will be carrying explosive cargos, and realize this, men, there are only a few inches of steel separating that cargo from enemy torpedoes and shells.

"There will be no sleeping while on watch, make no mistake. Take your duties seriously because every German and Japanese sailor wants to send you all to Davey Jones's locker. That's all men. Go below to your assigned bunks and await further orders."

This is the how the legacy of Jane Alice Peters (Carole Lombard) and Shad Whittington's destiny crossed paths.

The crew learned to respect and some loved their ship, almost as much as others admired the real Carole Lombard. I could only imagine that the crew was somewhat similar to the John Ford movie, *Mister Roberts,* wild and out of control at times yet they were just young men, scared and far away from home. None realized at the time the magnificent efforts and contributions they were making in the overall war effort.

Another front-porch swing story at 21 Linden Avenue included the trip to Murmansk, Russia, which, according to Pappy, was the coldest place on earth. You could see him tear up when he talked about the letters he got from the boys at the orphanage home.

In one such letter, JM wrote, "Daddy, we are being good boys, following the rules, we say our prayers every night. We just want to know when you will come back and get us out of here."

Those boys thought they had been placed in that home because they had done something wrong. They didn't understand they were victims of a bad marriage, and there was a war going on. When Pap told that story, it almost ripped my heart out.

One day at sea, after the *Carole Lombard* anchored, the men decided to go for a swim. Seamen not on duty started stripping down to their skivvies and jumping overboard. The crew was amazed when they saw Watts climb up on one of the ships booms, perform a precision high dive into the warm deep blue Pacific waters, then swim under the ship to surface on the other side.

Then the leaders on board started blowing whistles and throwing over rope ladders with voice commands sounded through megaphones to come aboard. Many in the water thought the ship was under attack, and after all were back on board, the duty officer pointed into the water and said, "Look down there."

The men were shocked when they saw an entire frenzy of tiger sharks swimming around the vessel. The deck officer said, "Some of you men don't have the sense God gave geese."

Pappy told me about how lonely he felt while standing bow watch one early morning. The crew was listening to a radio broadcast and started reminiscing about home. Then he saw the wake of what he thought was a sailfish off the starboard bow but suddenly realized it was the froth of a sixteen-foot Japanese torpedo. He sounded the alarm, and the ship maneuvered for evasive action.

They never spotted the submarine that launched the attack. The ironic part of these stories was in one instant, he was there on board the ship, wishing he was home. He was back on the *Carole Lombard* with just a thought. Pappy was so good at telling stories, we felt like we were on the deck with him and could feel the ship shudder when it hit a swell, hear the screws turning a stern, or feel the wind in our faces and almost smell the salt air.

Pappy was not a religious man, but his beliefs went much deeper than most realized. This became evident when he took a liberty and visited the Holy Lands. There, he walked the same path that Jesus took before being crucified, which left a profound impact on Shad Whittington.

Sometime in early 1945, while in a foreign port, Seaman Whittington was aware that America and its Allies were winning the war and wished the war to end quickly because his mother was not in very good health. While resting in a hotel room, he had a vivid dream about his mother Eva. He dreamed that she had died; the dream was so real he could see the blue coffin she was lying in and could visualize a messenger walking up the sidewalk, carrying a Western Union telegram stating that Eva Honeycutt Whittington had passed away. The dream woke Dad up, then he immediately went to the door, looked out the window, and saw the messenger carrying the very message that he had dreamed about. This was not a dream; it was a vision. Sadly, he was too far away to attend his mother's funeral.

Radio brought the servicemen news from around the world. The crew of the *Carole Lombard,* from time to time, could pick up announcements coming from Japan's radio propagandist, Tokyo Rose. She could get the crew so riled up; they would start cussing every time they heard her voice. After one radio broadcast, Seaman Whittington commented, "Somebody needs to hang that bitch."

Paul Azark added, "Not just somebody, if I have the chance, I would hang that lying bitch myself."

More bad news came over the radio waves when the crew and the rest of the nation learned that Pres. Franklin Delano Roosevelt died in Warm Springs, Georgia, on April 12, 1945. There were many Americans who did not agree with the president's progressive democratic New Deal policies, but he had been the president of the United States for twelve years, and most agreed that he was a great wartime president.

April happened to be a hell of a month for two dictators of the Tri-Axis group. Pappy's old nemesis since the second grade, Benito Mussolini, was caught while trying to escape with his mistress. The couple were shot, beaten to a pulp, and then hung upside down for public display on April 28, 1945. After hearing this news, the crew of the *Carole Lombard* became ecstatic and proclaimed, "They finally got that 'bawl'-headed bastard."

Two days later, on April 30, all the nations at war against the Tri-Axis powers were shocked when they heard that Adolph Hitler had committed suicide in a Berlin bunker. Oddly enough, Roosevelt and Hitler came in and out of power at almost the same time. Although the crew of the *Carole Lombard* was happier than ever before, they realized that the United States had to "whoop" Japan before they could go home. Despite this, most Americans could see a light at the end of the tunnel.

There was extensive planning that went into effect for the invasion of Japan. The greatest invasion of all time was postponed because of a secret project. What most didn't know at the time was on August 6, 1945, a B-29 was flying high overhead Hiroshima, Japan. The aircraft commander's name was Col. Paul Tibbets, and the Superfortress bore the name of Tibbet's mother, *Enola Gay.*

At 0815 hours, local Japanese time, the *Enola Gay* released the first atomic bomb that was ever dropped. The bombardier who pressed his eye to the Norden M series bombsight and held the plane steady during the bombing run was Thomas Ferebee from Mocksville, North Carolina.

Even after the devastation of the Hiroshima bomb, Japan refused to surrender. On August 9, another Superfortress named *Bockscar* dropped a plutonium bomb on Nagasaki. This led to Japan's formal surrender that took place aboard the USS *Missouri* in Tokyo Bay. The supreme commander of Allied Powers, Gen. Douglas MacArthur, presided over the ceremony, where the representatives of the Empire of Japan signed the Instrument of Surrender on September 2, 1945-World War 2 was over.

The news of the surrender marked a celebration by Americans and Allies alike that has not been equaled to this day. Ships at sea started blowing their whistles and turning their bows toward home.

The soldiers, airmen, marines, and sailors could not wait to get home.

Pap and others of his generation were part of the greatest conflict ever waged in the history of mankind. It has been estimated that 54 million lost their lives during this global conflict; of the 336,000 North Carolinians who joined, 9,000 lost their lives. Many Carolinians, like Pappy, were returning to their farms and fields, trying to pick up where they had left off. Others would have to start all over. Shad Whittington was coming back home to pick up the pieces of his life he had left behind.

Thirty-seven years after Carole Lombard's crash. I was an army aviator, Warrant Officer One (W-1), flying as a UH-1 copilot out of Las Vegas, Nevada, to Fort Irwin, California. As soon as we took off in aircraft 17539, Dave, the CW3 pilot in command, said, "Bill, I want to deviate south off course and show you something."

So after a few minutes, we came near Potosi pass, and Dave decelerated the helicopter to a hover, pointed to the huge black mark on Double Up Peak, and stated, "This is where Carole Lombard's DC-3 crashed into the rocks."

I remained silent while all those historical pieces of information began to line up, as if the aircraft we were flying had just become a time machine.

Chapter 20

Welcome Home

The mill hillers covered thousands of land, ai, and sea miles to arrive at what they called home, which was no different for Pappy's return. He had been out of touch with his hometown compadres since he joined and wondered what Concord and the surrounding area would be like.

His foremost thoughts were about the boys in the orphanage home, and other surviving family members. He wondered where he would find a job and if he could find a baseball team where he could add his name to the roster.

When Pap left the navy, he was thirty-one years old and at his physical peak, despite the thinning hair on top, the stomach operation where they removed an ulcer, and added a complete set of false teeth. A navy dentist had pulled his teeth during the run to Murmansk, Russia. His five-feet-eleven-inch, 190-pound frame sported a definite V-shaped upper torso, and he could do a chin-up with either hand. Coincidentally, America had reached the point where she was the most powerful and prosperous nation on earth.

Shad could hardly stay in his seat as the train neared the Concord train depot. When the train stopped at the station, other servicemen on the train waved their hands and said, "You are home, sailor, and my stop is just down the line. Hope to see you again sometime."

This was the same depot, right in front of the Cabarrus Mill, where he stood several years earlier and was bade a tearful departure granted by loving family members. However, when he arrived at the train station, no one was there to greet him.

The moment Pappy stepped out on the platform, he put his seabag and brown suitcase down then looked up and down the tracks. He was glad that his brother Will didn't show because Pappy would have probably wrung his neck, yet he realized that Will was not responsible for JM and Ted's future. Their future fell into Shad's hands and Shad's alone; besides, everyone in the Whittington family always felt sorry for Will. They called him poor old Willie.

As the passenger train pulled out of the station, servicemen were hanging out the windows, yelling many different goodbyes, such as "Come on over to Fayetteville, and I'll show you some good fishing spots."

One soldier stated, "Come to Lumberton, I am sure my sister would like to meet you," but the most proclaimed shout was, "Hey, Shad, why don't you visit my neck of the woods and show those boys how to hit home runs?"

The ones who didn't know him said, "Good luck in the future, sailor."

Pap would see some of those on that train again, but many would disappear into obscurity.

Pappy felt like a stranger in his hometown. He didn't have a car, so he hailed a cab and headed over to the Hotel Concord to get a room. After he got a whiff of Dutch Buffalo Creek, he realized the creek smelled just as bad as it did before. Yes, the place was the same, but he had changed. He viewed the world in a different light than ever before.

As soon as the cab driver saw Pap in his navy blues, he said, "The Shad Rack is back."

They knew each other and en-route to the hotel, exchanged bits and pieces of what had happened since he had been away. The cab driver said, "Oh lord, you won't believe how baseball has dropped off since you guys were away," and told how Gus Widenhouse's service station, just across the depot on the other side of 29A, blew up.

Things were changing by 1946. Hartsell and other Carolina schools had added a twelfth; whereas the year before, the students only had to attend eleven grades to receive a high school diploma. Hartsell and Winecoff schools were the first of the local county schools to have a football team in 1946.

A creek ran down the middle of the field behind Hartsell at the time, so Hartsell baseball games had to be played at the Brown Mill Ballpark.

The school systems were gearing up to provide the athletes of the future; whereas before, the majority of ballplayers were typically recruited from the textile and other industrial leagues. A spigot was added to the back of the mill houses on the Franklin Mill Hill, and the residents ran a hose from that spigot, which gave them the option to take cold showers in their garages, called car sheds.

Many across the nation, like in Cabarrus County, were eager to see baseball return to its former glory, but few could imagine just how big the baseball explosion was about to become. Shortly after WW2, North Carolina boasted to have more baseball leagues within its boundary than any other state.

After Pappy settled in at the hotel, he decided to stay around Concord for the next couple of days then arrange to have someone take him to Lincolnton to visit the boys and see his brother Clarence. He grew restless in his hotel room and decided to walk over to the Brown Mill Cafe and to his surprise, ran into several of the ballplayers returning from the war, and each had a story to tell.

The first guy he talked with was the nineteen-year-old knuckleball pitcher Howard Hooks. Howard dropped out of Hartsell School and like many others, fibbed about his age to get in the army. After Howard was inducted, he was sent as an enlisted man to Germany. The war in Europe was over, and he was assigned duties to guard and transport prisoners within the American sector.

Howard was a good-natured and jovial person, but when he got excited, he would speak in a high-pitched voice. He broke out laughing many times before he could tell Pappy about his war experience.

He said, "Shad, I was guarding these German prisoners in the back of this Deuce and a half (a two-and-a-half-ton truck). I was carrying a .30-caliber Carbine and was shooting out the lights on the poles as we drove by. Then the magazine fell out of my rifle, and those prisoners could hear my magazine bouncing down the road. They knew I was out of ammunition. So I turned and looked at those prisoners and ran my hand into my field jacket like I was reaching for a pistol. You know, Shad, those prisoners didn't even move." Then in his normal tone of voice, he added, "Shad, I think those people were plumb wore out. They were tired, hungry, and beaten and just wanted all the suffering to end."

Then Marvin Mauney, Willard's and Richard's younger brother, came in and pulled up a chair. All at the table shook hands with one another, and Marvin said, "Willard is back and will be here in a little while."

Then he told about his adventures while serving under General Patton. After they spoke about loved ones and future plans, the conversation shifted to baseball. Marvin then asked Pappy, "Did you hear about Richard going up to pitch for the Philadelphia Phillies?"

Shad took the lead when he said, "Why yes, Marvin, I saw Richard pitch in an exhibition game against the Yankees."

Richard's best pitch was a side-armed sinker, and according to Pappy, Richard could throw a baseball in a tomato can. In other words, he had excellent control.

The first time Joe came up to the plate, Richard struck him out. When DiMaggio came up during his second trip, Joe crowded the plate even more because Richard worked the outside corner of the plate the last trip. After Richard got two strikes on Joe, he whipped a side-armed sinking fast ball on the inside corner, Joe hit a slow roller back up the middle to Richard, and as Richard fielded the ground ball, he told Joe DiMaggio as he was running to first base, "You ain't nothing but a big name."

When DiMaggio came up to the plate the third time, Richard's team was winning the game, 4 to 3. Richard had to pitch from the stretch because there was a runner on second. Richard fired two more strikes that struck their mark on the outside corner, and Joe was still crowding the plate. Richard took the signal from the catcher, went into his stretch, checked the runner at second, then turned to fire his in-shoot sinker on the inside corner, and realized that Joe had backed off the plate. Pappy said, "He could see Joe's home run splash into the bay." Richard's team lost 5 to 4.

Pappy told Marvin, "If Richard had not made that wisecrack to Joe, Richard might have won the game."

Richard Mauney happened to be the only baseball player from the Franklin Mill Hill who made it to the Major Leagues.

Before the guys left the Brown Mill Cafe, Johnson Strube walked in, and he had the most shocking war story of them all. Johnson was a young soldier who had been captured by the Germans and was scared out of his wits during his interrogation. He was just a country boy far away from home. After harsh questioning, the German interrogator said, "You are of no use to us, prisoner. We know more about your unit and its mission than you do."

Johnson said, "They herded the prisoners into boxcars, and while the train was en route, American planes flew overhead and started strafing our train, thinking it was loaded with ammunition." Then Johnson added, "Those Germans let our planes do their killing for them. It just so happened that bullets ripped through the latch of our boxcar door, and we busted the door open and leaped out that door as fast as we could."

Shad, Marvin, and Howard just looked at Johnson without saying a word. Then Johnson added with tears in his eyes, "Shad, I don't know how many men were killed that day on the train." Johnson Strube told me the same story almost word for word at my house many years later.

Pap broke the melancholy mood with, "Well, it's over now, Johnson, and I am glad you are back. Who are you going to pitch for this season?"

Johnson had the most powerful arm on the Franklin Mill Hill. Many on the hill swore they saw Johnson throw an Irish potato from Dabbs Grocery store and hit the Franklin Mill. The distance is so far, I would have to see an event like this to believe it.

Johnson had very little control over his pitches and was considered quite wild. Pappy caught Johnson from time to time and said, "I went out to the mound during one game to pay Johnson a visit and told him, 'Look, Johnson, so far, you have walked four and hit five other batters. Right now, we are ahead, 6 to 5, and if you'd settle down and start throwing strikes, we might just win this game.'

It didn't take long for Pappy to link up with those who had returned from service, and word spread that Shad was back but wasn't going to stay in Concord very long. He linked up with Boyd Lee who offered to give Pappy a ride to Lincolnton to see Clarence and visit the boys. Boyd told Shad he would do it for a few dollars plus meals.

When Boyd dropped him off at Clarence's place, Pap arranged for Boyd to pick him up in a week to drive him back to Concord. Many servicemen returning from the war hitchhiked or thumbed their way across the state, and drivers were glad to give those returning servicemen rides and listen to their wartime adventures.

When Clarence saw his youngest brother in the driveway, he said, "Come on in, Pete."

Clarence called Pappy Pete, just like Mr. Frank did when Father was a twelve-year-old working at the Franklin. Regretfully, I never found out why.

After Beulah fixed them a meal, they gabbed out on the porch for a while then headed down to the spring and started pitching horseshoes. Both men were excellent horseshoe pitchers, and if one made a mistake, the other would make short work of the game. This reminds me of the games I saw them play against each other when we used to visit Uncle Clarence.

This scene was the same when Pap and Uncle Clarence pitched horseshoes in the same location in 1946. During their games, Pappy worked out the details for future plans, which they had discussed while the games were being played. Pap was going to visit JM and Ted, return to Concord, and try to make some money, working in the mill and playing baseball. After the '46 season was over, he would move in with Clarence, take a textile or carpentry job around Lincolnton, and try to get on one of the teams in the Western Carolina League. This would give him a chance to spend more time with his boys.

The boys jumped for joy when they saw their father for the first time in years. They thought a magnificent white knight had just ridden in on a powerful draft horse and was going to throw them up on his saddle and ride away. However, this was merely a visit that would only offer another tearful departure at the end of the session.

Shad Whittington didn't have a steady job, home, vehicle, or a place for the boys to live. He painfully explained to the boys they were better off where they were; they were being fed, cared for, and getting an education, a chance that he never had.

When Boyd Lee came by to take him back to Concord the next day, Pappy was kind of down in the dumps, and Boyd noticed he wasn't his usual self, so on the way back to Concord, they talked about things that weren't so painful. Boyd Lee told Brother Ted many years later, "Shad Whittington paid me a lot of money in those days to carry him around from place to place."

Shad worked part time as a carpenter and full time at the Brown Mill. He decided he would rally several of the ballplayers whom he used to play for and against and finish out the 1946 season in style. The first guy he linked up with was Big George Hatley who used to pitch for the Cabarrus Mill. Then he got the knuckleball pitcher Howard Hooks excited about playing because Shad would prefer to have those two pitchers on his side rather than having to bat against them. He even talked the hard-throwing right-handed Reed Gown into playing for this pick-up team. Father said that "Reed Gown had a drop that looked like it fell off the table, just as the batter started his swing."

Another player who was added to the fold was Vernon Ford, the big right-handed power hitter. The only missing piece was a manager that had the clout to rally the rest of the team. Miraculously, Pete DiMizio volunteered for the job.

Pete was of Italian descent and spoke English with a heavy Italian accent. He loved the game of baseball, and it was reported that Pete was an excellent organizer, would bet heavily on the games, but paid his ballplayers well, especially if Pete won the bets. Pete recruited the remainder of the players, and now they were ready to wreak havoc for the rest of the 1946 season.

The team decided to play a tune-up game in Hamlet, North Carolina, just on the other side of Rockingham. Sunday baseball could be played there with not as much fall-out from the blue laws that prevailed in Cabarrus County. A young Bill Ford, a junior at Hartsell School at the time, was added to the roster.

The team could not afford a bus, so the players had to carpool to and from Concord in an amazing array of vehicles. Having a vehicle that ran properly was a premium because some of the players worked the third shift at their mills and had to be back ready to work at eleven o'clock that night. Many players did not own cars, and the few who had vehicles, as the ballplayers would say, "was not in good shape." It would be taken for granted today how long the trip would have taken.

Only two-lane roads existed at the time, and the convoy of ballplayers would have to come to a stop at each little town they passed. This was long before the interstate system was developed. Eventually, they arrived and started piling out of their cars, grabbing and unloading equipment, then started warming up.

Hamlet had an old-style ball field, no fence nor lights, and in no time at all, the game got underway. Howard Hooks was coaching first base, and his goal was to alert the hitters the best he could by picking up the signals from the catcher or by closely monitoring any nuances the pitcher might yield before he threw a certain pitch.

Howard and Vernon worked out a system in advance. If the pitcher was going to throw a curve, Howard would say, "Come on, Pinto."

The verbal signal for a change-up was "What you say, Ford?"

And if it was a fast ball, Howard would say, "Come on, Uncle Vernon."

The other team didn't have a clue.

The highlight of the game was when Vernon came up to bat, and immediately, Howard chimed in with his high-pitched voice, "Come on, Uncle Vernon."

It was a challenge with a hard-throwing right-handed pitcher facing a hard-low fast-ball hitter. As soon as Vernon made perfect contact with the ball, the people could not believe what they saw. Everybody there that day said that that was the longest hit ball than anybody had seen in their entire life. The ball went to straightaway center field and bounced in between the doors of a barn. Shad said, "You could have hung a month's washing on that line drive."

A line drive in those days was called a clothes' line drive. The game had to be delayed because they didn't have any additional baseballs, and all three of the Hamlet outfielders scoured through the barn until they found the baseball.

After the game, players donated gas money to the drivers, which would have been a mere pittance in those days but still relative to the wages earned. The players who had to work the third shift traded seats and rode back in the fastest cars. When Bill Ford got back to his house on Robinson Street, his mother sat him down at the table and said, "As long as you live in this house, I don't want you to play ball on Sundays."

Roberta was the name of the textile mill located just on the north side of Coddle Creek. The mill was constructed in 1906 and was reported to have been named after the daughter of the man who built the mill. A little mill community sprung up around this textile mill, nestled in between Concord and Harrisburg, North Carolina.

Most of the ballplayers from Shad's era said that Roberta had a baseball field as far back as they could remember. This was one of the baseball fields where Shad earned his nickname. Most people also agreed that the Roberta community hated to lose and if visiting teams won, would have to fight their way off the field and out through the parking lot. This rivalry was even worse than the Kannapolis Towlers and the Concord Weavers because Roberta fans were indiscriminate; they hated all the other ball teams. Most teams could expect a fight if they played on the Roberta Baseball Field.

The first game was set, and Pete's team was ready to play against Roberta. George Hatley was pitching, and Shad was catching. Pete's team scored a couple of runs in the first inning, and Big George went out to take the mound for Pappy's team. The only problem was the plate umpire, whose real name was never established; the ballplayers called him Pear Shape because he was rather large and shaped like a pear.

George reared back and let loose a fast ball right down the middle; the batter didn't swing because the ball came in so fast, but the plate umpire bellowed, "Ball."

Shad said, "Come on, that was right down the middle."

Right then, the visiting team suspected that Pear Shape had bet on the game for Roberta. George repeated his first pitch that came in even harder, the batter left his bat on his shoulder, and the pitch crossed the heart of the plate for a second time. Pear Shape yelled, "Ball two!"

It was already too late. Shad threw off his mask and tried to intercept a mad six-foot-six George Hatley who was covering the distance between the mound and home plate faster than one could imagine; George stepped around Pappy and knocked Pear Shape out with a left hook. The base umpire came up and threw George out of the game. Reed Gown had to finish the game, but Pappy's team ended up beating Roberta that day.

Howard Hooks was slotted to pitch against Roberta the next scheduled game, and while Howard was warming up, the on-deck Roberta hitter knocked the catcher out after he threw the ball down to second base before he had a chance to put his mask on. Father ran in from right field and stood behind Howard and said, "I got your back, Howard."

Nobody charged the mound because they didn't want any part of Shad Whittington, nor Howard for that reason, because Howard had the game ball in his hand. It is not very wise to charge the mound if the pitcher has a baseball in his hand.

Hank Utley, the coauthor of "The Independent Carolina Baseball League," offered his Roberta experience. Hank's father told him, "Boy, when you play at Roberta, whatever you do, don't say anything to the Roberta team or the spectators. After the game is over, go straight to your car and leave."

Hank happened to be playing third base against Roberta one Saturday, when he just could not take it anymore. The Roberta team was sitting on the bench, right beside Utley, and there was a row of cedar trees just behind the Roberta bench. Hank broke his silence with the Roberta team and said, "I don't know about you guys, but something is tearing my neck up."

One Roberta player said, "Yeah, we know. You see that boy with his BB gun in the cedar behind us? He has been shooting you in the neck since the third inning."

The Roberta players were quite civil and were generally not the cause of the unruly behavior; the trouble was caused by drunken and aggressive spectators. It was shocking to experience a small rural community exploding over a baseball game. Usually, when fights broke out, the ballplayers would just sit down on a base or in their respective positions in the field until the dispute was settled.

Pap's team was scheduled to play their last game that season against Roberta. The night before the game, Shad, Vernon Ford, and Howard Hooks stayed out late, drinking until the wee hours of the morning. When Vernon Ford stepped into the batter's box during the game, the pitcher unleashed a high fast-ball. Vernon swung at it and missed by about a foot and fell down beside home plate. Pete DiMizio looked at his ballplayers on the bench and in his heavy Italian English accent asked, "What's a wrong-a-with Verna?"

Shad and Howard dropped their heads and started laughing, and Howard added, "I guess Vernon is not feeling too good today, Pete."

Later on in the game, Roberta started losing, and this gave rise to a wave of spectator unrest. As mentioned previously, Shad was in excellent shape and could still do a chin-up with either hand because he maintained his calisthenics routine after he left the navy. He had sailed around the world twice and was angered by how the Roberta spectators were messing up the game of baseball. It would only take one more situation, and he would release the flood waters of the Nile River.

That came shortly after three drunk self-proclaimed badasses started harassing the team's beloved manager, Pete DiMizio. The final straw came when one of the ruffians grabbed Pete by the face and pushed him down by the bench. Shad threw off his catcher's mask, sprinted over to the perpetrator at Mauney speed, spun the guy around, and dropped him with a straight right hand. Immediately, the second fellow threw a haymaker at Shad, which Shad ducked under and answered with a left hook that sent the second troublemaker knocked out cold to the ground. The third guy tried to run but didn't make it very far. Shad got him in a half-Nelson, a move he learned from his navy buddy, Paul Azark, then spun him around a couple of times and threw the guy over the fence into a pigpen beside the ball field.

Then Pappy said, "Stay in there, you are not fit to be around humans." Pap turned to the Roberta players and fans and yelled, "Do you want to fight or play baseball?"

They answered, "Hell, Shad, we want to play baseball."

Then the Roberta fans started laughing because the pig walked over to the guy Shad threw into the pen and just looked at him as if to say, "What are you doing in here with me?"

After the season was over, several of the ballplayers invited Shad to go dove-hunting. Pappy hunted and fished with most of the players, but he wasn't too keen on dove-hunting. While hunting at the edge of an open field, a dole of dove flew over their position, and Shad let loose with the right-hand barrel of his side-by-side double-barreled shotgun and dropped the first bird.

His second shot only winged the next dove. What happened next shocked everybody there because after the wounded dove hit the ground, Father said, "The bird ran around me a couple of times, dragging one of its wings, making an awful noise." Shad emptied his gun, slammed the breach closed, and added, "That's it for me, boys, I am done." He started to walk away, but after he took a few steps, he turned back toward his hunting group and said, "It's a sin to kill a dove."

Later in life, he told me the story about Noah and the ark and what happened after Noah released the dove.

Chapter 21

Morganton – Mount Pleasant and Mae Belle

When the snow finally melted around Lincolnton, by early March, changes had taken place. Shad had taken several trips to and from Concord throughout the winter and had jobs lined up in Lincolnton and Morganton. During that off season, the right-handed Fred Parnell from the Norcott Mill team wanted Shad to play baseball with his team in Morganton. Fred had spoken highly of Shad's ball-playing ability to Aggie Beach, the owner of the Morganton Aggies. It happened to be the same year that Branch Rickie signed Jackie Robinson with the Brooklyn Dodgers. Bill (Duck) Ford graduated from Hartsell High School and had signed with a Minor League team out of Muncie, Indiana, associated with the Cincinnati organization.

Big George Hatley also wanted Shad to play for his class D baseball team in Landis. Shad reluctantly declined the offer and told George he really would like to play for Landis but wanted to be near his boys in the orphanage.

Shad joined the Morganton Aggies in 1947, and after completing spring training, the Aggies were scheduled to play their opening night game in Davidson, North Carolina. They were to face the renowned left-handed power pitcher Billy Joe Davis. Shad was not yet known in the western part of the state, and the fans didn't know what to think of this newcomer.

When Pappy walked up to the plate for his first time with the Aggies, before he stepped into the batter's box, he held his bat by the maul, bent over slightly, threw the handle or the knob of the bat against the plate, and the bat bounced off the plate right back into Shad's hands, the proper way a batter should hold the bat. He then placed his bat calmly on his shoulder as he stood up in the batter's box.

The crowd wondered why this new arrival would display such confidence for his first time at bat. They didn't have to wait long because the first pitch that Billy Joe Davis threw, a fast ball on the inside corner, and as the old expression goes, Pappy hit the ball nine miles out of the ballpark. The line drive was climbing like a golf ball as it cleared the right field fence, and the ball hit way up and bounced off the National Guard Armory building. Those mountain people remarked, "Shad Whittington could hit a baseball so far that it looked like an aspirin tablet."

Needless to say, he got off to a good start in the Western Carolina League.

The Morganton Aggies were a good team and played very aggressive baseball. There was a mental hospital located in Morganton at the time, and it was reported by opposing team members that some of the Aggie players were patients from that mental hospital because they played like crazy people.

Shad made mincemeat out of most of the pitchers in the Western Carolina League, and they were scheduled to play against the Forest City Owls. I have heard this story told many times, but the most memorable rendition came from Eddie Kennedy, when he worked at the Jackson Park barbershop.

Eddie said, "Shad was waiting to get his haircut and told us about the first game he played against Forest City. Shad said they had to wait a while before the game started because the Forest City pitcher had not showed up yet. Then we saw someone way down yonder in the valley walking through the cornfields, wearing a Forest City uniform."

The Aggies noticed that when the player stepped out from the edge of the cornfield, he was as tall as the cornstalks around him. The Aggie team kept eyeing this long and slender pitcher, wearing his baseball uniform, baseball uniform with a long-sleeved jersey shirt underneath. As he strode toward the Forest City bench, his stirrup socks were rolled up to his knees, and he was barefooted. He was wearing his glove on his left hand and had his spikes tied together thrown over his left shoulder.

As soon as he got to the bench, he sat down and threw his spikes on the ground, wiped his feet with a towel, then put on a pair of white socks, plus a pair of sanitary socks, and stretched his stirrup socks over his heels. Then he put on his spikes and laced them up tight. A fellow at the end of the bench opened a box and pulled out the game ball and tossed it to the pitcher. The team's catcher stepped out in front of the bench to warm up the pitcher, and the Aggies noticed the pitcher they were going to face only threw eight warm-up pitches and then motioned that he was ready to start.

One of the Aggie players asked, "What do you think, Shad?"

Pappy replied, "We will knock that damn hillbilly back into the mountains."

The Morganton Aggies were about to meet Phil Oats. Shad told the Aggies, "There is not a right-hander in this league that I cannot hit."

That night Shad was about to be proven wrong because Phil Oats slammed the door in the Aggies' faces by pitching a shut-out.

Pap said Phil Oats was so tall, it looked like he could almost hand the ball to the catcher, that he caught a glimpse of Phil's fast-ball then heard the umpire scream, "Strike one!"

Pap stepped out of the box and said, "I don't know, Mr. Ump, it sounded pretty low when it went by."

The umpire chuckled then said, "Get back in there and hit, Whittington."

Pappy went on to say, "Phil's next pitch was the best change-up he had ever seen, and the pitch after that was a fast curve ball that broke about three inches, just enough to make me miss the ball." Pap concluded, "I came up to bat twenty-two times against Phil Oats that season and only got one sorry hit, a 'dying seagull' over the second baseman's head from a check swing."

This roguish meandering from Concord to Morganton, Lincolnton, and back seemed straightforward; however, a strong and loving partner was missing in Shad's life. Although baseball was his first love, yet despite having an excellent season with the Aggies in 1947, he decided not to return to the Morganton Aggies in 1948.

The Morganton Aggies team upgraded from semipro status to a class D Minor League team in 1948. Many of Shad's friends, especially Fred Parnell, who stayed with the Aggies and ascended the Minor League baseball rungs of the ladder, could not determine why a player with Shad's ability would not venture past the semipro level, probably the same question George Hatley asked Shad when he refused to play for Landis the season prior.

Shad never gave a specific reason to anyone why he made the decision to stay within the semipro level. There were certain baseball facts that would have to be considered in the world of baseball at that time.

There were six different Minor League baseball levels, which included Classes D, C, B, A or A1, AA, and AAA, then the Major Leagues. A player would not have to progress through all those levels, depending on the player's ability. In other words, a player could come from a class D level and proceed directly to the majors, but that was rare.

Conversely, a player could also spend his entire career climbing this baseball ladder and not make it to the show (the Major Leagues). It must also be known that most baseball players endeavored to make it to the Majors.

At the time there were only sixteen teams in the Major Leagues with about twenty players to each roster, so the vertical ascent would have been slow. A player could spend most of his career within the Minor Leagues. Another fact that might have influenced Pappy's decision was the Minor League structure. Usually, the higher the rung or tier, the farther the team would have to travel to play, which meant more time away from home.

WW2 enabled Pappy to travel the world over, so traveling was not a problem; however, those war years happened to coincide during his prime baseball years of consideration. A player might forgo all the travel involved and still play good baseball at the semipro level by staying local.

The most important consideration was that Shad happened to be thirty-two years old at the time and would have been considered over the hill, too old for the Majors. You would be surprised at how many of Shad's peers from the Carolina Textile baseball leagues would end up making the same decision Shad made.

The Mount Pleasant team picture, like other photos of semipro teams, will show many uniform variations; whereas Minor or Major League teams would have matching uniforms. The uniform consisted of a baseball cap, a baggy short-sleeved jersey, with matching baggy pants made of wool, preferably a black belt, and those ugly old wool stirrup socks with horizontal white stripes.

Semipro teams could not afford standardized uniforms, and if a player was added to the roster later in the season, that player would have to make up the difference by acquiring a similar uniform through a local sporting goods store.

When I played for Hartsell School twenty years later, I wore the same styled red and gray baggy wool uniform. It wasn't until I played for Central Cabarrus High School in the late '60s when we were issued much-nicer tighter-fitting uniforms made of polyester material. The polyester uniforms looked much better and fit tighter than the old-style uniforms. The modern uniforms were made of thin material and would rip more easily after sliding on hard dirt, which would cause strawberries to form on the legs or the rump. I preferred to wear the older-style uniform because of that reason alone.

When Shad played for Mount Pleasant, it gave him a chance to reunite with his baseball mentor, Herman "Ginger" Watts, who happened to be the team manager. The ballplayers called him Ginger. Ginger Watts lived in Mount Pleasant at the time, and his home sported a wooden fence that consisted of old baseball bats instead of boards.

Shad moved back to Concord and resided in an apartment on 22 Valley Street and went back to work at the Brown Mill. He played ball for the mill during the regular season but played tournament baseball with Mount Pleasant or Pete DiMizio's traveling team.

One of the highest-scoring games occurred during a pick-up game one weekend at Brown Mill Baseball Park. Pete's team slaughtered an opposing team, and it was stated that everyone in the lineup hit a home run that day. Howard Hooks, the pitcher, who did not consider himself to be a good hitter, batted a thousand, including a single, two doubles, a triple, and a home run. Shad hit four consecutive home runs and made the splinters fly off the right center field wall during his fifth trip to the plate. He came so close to hitting five home runs in one game, which would have been a baseball first. Pete's team was still batting when the game was called on account of darkness. This was just another day in baseball paradise, however, there was something missing in Shad's life, which happened to be a special woman who would be willing to share her life with his.

Mae Belle standing in the Goodman front yard circa 1947

Shad visited his brother Willie several times during the 1948 season. Will happened to be living at the Old Fink Place in China Grove at the time. During one visit, he happened to notice a rather tall and lanky woman with dark brown hair, working in a field nearby. He asked Willie if he knew anything about the woman, and Will said, "She is William Goodman's daughter, and I think her name is Mae Belle."

Mae Belle was the third child, the first girl born to William Thomas and Ida Roseman Goodman, of which seven other siblings would follow. These are some of the things that Mae's younger sister, Carrie, had to say. "Even when Mae was a young woman, she would hook the up the horse, drive the wagon to the end of Daughtery Road, and harvest the corn." They called it pulling roastnears. "After her wagon was full, she would drive the horse and wagon back to the barn, unhook, feed and water the horse, and unload the wagon. She culled the ears of corn by placing the good ears in one bin (the ones meant for people), and the others were stored in a bin that were used for the cattle, horses, and pigs."

Carrie added, "When Mae was old enough to work in the mill, she would start her day by hooking up the horse to the wagon, loading a plow in the back of the wagon. She would drive to whichever field that needed to be plowed, unload the plow, unhook the horse from the wagon, and hook him up to the plow.

"Mae Belle could plow like a man, and when finished plowing, she would unhook the plow, reharness the horse to the wagon, load the plow, and drive back to the barn. After she put the horse in the barn, she would wash up by the well, get her a bite to eat, change her clothes, and walk to the intersection of Lent and Daughtery Road in time enough to catch the mill bus that would take her to Plant 1 in Kannapolis.

"She worked the second shift in the mill, 3:00-11:00 p.m. At the end of her shift, she would catch the mill bus that would drop her off at the end of Daugherty Road, where she would walk home in the dark."

This process was repeated again and again, except on Sundays.

Mae attended a one-room classroom on Lentz Road just across the street from where she would later catch the mill bus. She, like Shad, only finished the sixth grade because she was needed to help farm the fifty-three-acre Goodman spread.

Mae was also an excellent cook. The Goodman girls were taught to sew, knit, crochet, and quilt, and they could out-work most men in the field. The women in the Goodman family not only grew garden vegetables; they also had a special talent for maintaining beautiful flower gardens.

Shad asked Will to put in a good word for him about his desire to see Mae. There were many similarities between Shad and Mae; Both were lonely, they were hard workers that understood agriculture, both worked in the textile industry-Shad ran slubbers, cards, and hoppers; and Mae worked in the sheet department at Plant 1 in Kannapolis.

There were also several differences between the two; Mae was raised in a large close-knit family, devout Lutherans, whereas the Whittingtons were heavy drinkers and hell-raisers. The Goodman family could care less about anything sports related and had probably never even seen a baseball game.

Shad Whittington had to be at his best behavior just to get to the Goodman front door. Will and his wife Nanny did put in good word for Shad, and despite the couple's differences, William and Ida Goodman allowed Shad to visit and date their daughter.

When Shad made his introduction to the Goodman family, he used his proper name, Jim, instead of his baseball nickname. The couple's first few dates consisted of just sitting and talking in the front yard on the cool summer grass. They discussed whatever was on their minds underneath a shade tree at the edge of the flower garden, and they took strolls along the driveway that ran from the house to Daugherty Road. They talked about their dreams and what they expected from each other.

Mae called him Jim at first and later more intimately, Jimmie. But if she was irritated with him, she called him James, and when she was really upset, she used his full name, James Manual Whittington, as if it were official.

Jim impressed Mae during their walks because he knew the common name of every tree they passed and made comments, such as, "Look at that old post oak, I wonder just how old this tree is. If that tree could talk, I'll bet it could tell some wonderful stories, and look at that tall lazy sycamore leaning across the branch."

When they walked through the flower garden Mae had the advantage. The Goodman flower garden was quite impressive, and Jim would try to name a particular flower. Mae would just laugh and then tell him the flower's proper name.

Shad remained in the apartment at 22 Valley Street in Concord during the 1948 baseball season. He played baseball in various towns, visited the boys in the orphanage, and saw Mae whenever he could. It wasn't until he was invited by the Goodman family one evening for homemade ice cream that he told her about his two sons from a previous marriage, who happened to be staying in Cypes Orphanage Home near Lincolton. This news did not deter

Mae one bit because she was quite taken by this ballplayer. After this important date, they started writing each other.

I am fortunate to have some of the letters they exchanged, and I would like to paraphrase what was contained in some of those letters. The first letter Shad sent was scribed on the top right portion of the page, "April 25, '49, Concord, NC."

The main body was short and sweet and began with, "Dearest Darling, I thought I would drop you a line. I hope everything is going fine-with me, not so hot-after meeting you last Sunday, I can't get you off my mind. I'll have you know that I had a swell time when I was near you."

He ended the letter with, "Hope to see you soon. Sign Jim."

Mae's return letter did not have a date in the right-hand column, just "Thursday Morning," and the letter began with, "Dearest Darling: Just got back from the mailbox and what do you think I got-nothing more than a sweet and welcomed letter from you, dear. Sure was glad to hear from you."

His next letter was dated May 2, 1949, and was more intimate. He wrote, "Honey, I got home okay! But, darling, it was awful lonesome going down that old lonely road. But do you think I would mind that? Honey, I would walk down a hundred lonely roads for you."

The next line started with "Darling, good night," then a few lines below that was "LOTS OF LOVE," printed in big letters, and he ended the letter with, "Sign Jim."

He apologized for not having much of an education in some of his letters and indicated that was why he wrote his letters in pencil, so if he made a mistake, he could rub it out, ha ha.

Mae always wrote in ink. She would kid him about the how he misspelled *gir; gril* was how he spelled it. He told her in one letter that he had been approached by other teams to play baseball in the eastern part of the state and in South Carolina, of which he declined. He told them he had met a wonderful woman and could not travel far away.

In another letter, he had considered joining the merchant marines, until he met her. I was quite surprised when I read, "I have been with a lot of girls, some of them thought they were movie stars, and you can't love a girl like that."

But the most shocking line was, "Honey, I am no Christian, but I thank God for having you."

He included that he wanted her to just show up one day in the stands, and just knowing that she was there would make him hit better. This is reminiscent of a scene in a movie that I saw called *The Natural*, when Iris Gaines, played by Glenn Close, showed up at the ballpark to see Roy Hobbs (The Natural) played by Robert Redford.

A critical scene in the movie was when Roy Hobbs stepped into the batter's box for his third trip to the plate. He had struck out the two previous trips and was in a terrible slump. Then Iris stood up in the stands, and he stepped out of the batter's box as if he could feel her presence, then he stepped back in to the batter's box and settled down. During the next pitch, you could hear the crack of the bat, and his home run shattered a clock in center field. That scene had a powerful reference and a significant parallel to the letter I just described. Those letters remained locked away in a cedar chest for forty-seven years, and I consider myself to be very fortunate to have those letters in my possession.

Jim and Mae decided to marry, and they were wed on June 10 in York County, South Carolina. It was common to travel across the South Carolina state line to tie the knot because they didn't have, to wait for the blood work to return, which was required by North Carolina law. There were two Concord baseball players who witnessed and signed the marriage certificate, and they were Glenn Kindley and Big George Hatley. This is how Shad met Mae Belle, and I will have you know that wonderful woman Mae Whittington would later become my mother.

Chapter 22

A Fresh Start in Rowan County

The couple moved into a four-room house, complete with indoor plumbing on four acres of land. The property was situated alongside Lentz Road, right up the road where Mae Belle caught the mill bus. She had worked this property while growing up, and this parcel of land was promised to be hers after she wed.

By this time, the road system was improving dramatically, and the influx of vehicles were populating the streets at an alarming rate. Thanks in part to the GI Bill, housing projects were appearing where only woodlands and open fields used to exist. The postwar boom was in swing.

For the first time in his life. Shad lived in a house he could call his own and was very proud of this instant promotion. He was privileged enough to pull his boys out of the orphanage home. He went to work for a textile mill in China Grove and played baseball for Salisbury. The story seemed to unfold with fairy-tale-like qualities, yet this was no fairy tale, and hidden strife began to surface.

There were four different people, strangers to one another, living in the same house, each confronted with new expectations.

The boys had been part of a strict, organized orphanage environment for the umpteen years and did not seem to fit in. While the newlyweds were enthralled with each other, the boys felt they were left out or simply in the way. So there were times when the boys felt more comfortable when they stayed with their uncles, Will or Clarence, which happened a lot.

The eldest son, JM, was fifteen years old, and Ted was thirteen, just coming of age. Now they had more free time and less oversight, which led to more adolescence. JM had waited for so many years for his father to show up and by this time had lost hope and was quite bitter by the way things turned out.

Ted, on the other hand, was more happy-go-lucky and took things more in stride. Nonetheless, he felt the pains of being separated from his loved ones just as much. Ted learned at this early age how to hide anguish and turn despair into humor, one of the greatest gifts ever given to a human being. Furthermore, unlike Shad's era, school attendance was now mandatory, so the boys had to be enrolled into a local school at the equivalent education level they had received at the orphanage.

Mae continued to work hard as ever, around the house and in the mill, even though she was pregnant with her first child. Then tragedy struck; Mae's little girl, Gerldine, was stillborn. The family had a tearful ceremony and buried her in the local cemetery. This event almost destroyed the family. Shad started drinking harder than ever. Just when family misery seemed to be at its peak, the nation was about to take another plunge on the international scene.

On June 25, 1950, the separate spheres of influences gave way on the Korean Peninsula. Kim Il-Sung's forces crossed the 38th parallel and deliberately attacked Syngman Rhee's South Koreans. The Korean War had started. President Truman announced that American forces would be committed to the Korean Peninsula, not for war, but to intervene on behalf of the United Nations as a police action.

"God Almighty, will it ever end?" cried Shad and other WW2 veterans who swore there would never be another war, especially after the one they had just experienced.

Many from Shad's group, including Willard and Marvin Mauney, Bill and Howard Hooks, were not recalled for military action. However, Bill Ford was drafted into the army.

Shad continued pursuing the only consistent stabilizing force in his life, and that was playing baseball. Around this time, Shad played baseball for the Salisbury Bombers in the Yadkin Valley League. A young and upcoming ballplayer, Harold Furr, from Roberta started playing alongside Shad. Harold was a farmer, strong as an ox, so strong they nicknamed him the Bull. The Bombers went to bat against a young and upcoming pitcher named Hoyt Wilhelm out of Mooresville, North Carolina.

Power hitters really hated to bat against knuckleball pitchers of any sort. Pappy stated that Hoyt wore his baseball cap down over his ears, and he looked so young; he wondered if his mama knew he was out so late. Then he added Hoyt had the best butterfly pitch he had ever seen.

Howard Hooks, the Franklin Mill knuckleballer, got his Minor League debut with the Concord Weavers in 1951. Unfortunately, his Minor League career was short-lived. Howard had a tendency to play outside of his Minor League contract to pick up additional money, and one night, during a game he was pitching in Albermarle, a batter hit a line drive up the middle, and the ball hit Howard right in the forehead. The line drive dropped him in front of the mound as if he had been shot with a rifle. The baseball knocked him silly, and everyone who saw the play was surprised the line drive didn't kill him. Howard recovered somewhat and wanted to stay in and pitch, but the manager took him out of the game.

From that point on, Howard was gun shy and wanted to lie down behind the mound after every pitch for fear of being hit. This phobia ruined his chance of progressing through the ranks to play better baseball. Howard told me years later, "If they would have let me stay in the game, I would have worked through that mess." Then he went on to say, "What really upset me was I didn't get to finish the game and get the $100 I was promised."

HORSHOE FOR GOOD LUCK – Manager "Shad" Whittington of the Salisbury Bombers second from left, is shown above shortly after he was presented a horseshoe of flowers for good luck in the Yadkin Valley League this season. Shown with him are clown "Skin" Alexander, left, Whittington, sponsor Pete DiMizio and Spencer Manager Lester Smith. (Photo by Johnny Suther)

Shad's 1951 baseball season consisted of playing less and organizing more. He moved from out behind the plate into right-field because it was less wear and tear on the body. He enjoyed being the skipper of the Salisbury Bomber All Stars and would take his team throughout the state to play tournament baseball. During one tournament, the Bombers were tied with a fierce opponent in extra innings, when Saint Louis Slugger, Enos Slaughter, came up to bat. The infield was playing in, and Slaughter drove a shot through the Salisbury Bomber shortstop, who happened to be Thurman (Punch) Ford, Bill Ford's younger brother. That crucial hit beat the Bombers, 4 to 3, and Slaughter's team went on to play in the regional tournament in Kansas City.

This story has always confused me because Enos Slaughter was still on the Saint Louis Cardinal roster and would have been overqualified to play down at the semipro level, but I guess stranger things have happened in the baseball world.

The Bombers won the 1951 Roxboro Tournament; the team photo featured a fifteen-year-old Ted Whittington as the team's bat boy. Shad would be thirty-seven at the end of the '51 season, and that was considered old for a baseball player. His age, coupled with his hard lifestyle, plus working the third shift at the cotton mill, was taking their physical and mental tolls.

The travel to and from the tournaments was worrisome; this left little time for anything to go wrong. A person could lose their job if they didn't make it back to work on time. When Pappy was telling me about those days, he relayed something to me that I think about to this day. He said, "Life is a battle between what we would like to do and the things we must do." I think that struggle has been felt by us all.

There was a ceremony at the Salisbury Baseball Park to wish Shad good luck during the '51 season as the Bombers' player/manager, complete with a live radio broadcast of the event. The local newspaper captured a snapshot with Pete DiMizio and Shad. They presented him with a horseshoe of flowers, which was considered a high baseball honor.

Sometime during the 1952 season, Shad told the Bombers he had had enough. He also indicated this in a letter he had written to Mae, stating, "I told Gibby and Watts, I don't play baseball to fill the stands, I play baseball to win."

This philosophy rang true about everything he did. Baseball was not just a game to him; it was a way of life.

Shad left Rowan County and the Salisbury Bombers because he had picked out a piece of land on Linden Avenue, two streets over from Union Cemetery Road, just south of Coley Airport. The property was only 3/10 of a mile from where Pappy was born. He also bought a new 1952 Blue Crown Victoria Ford and enrolled JM and Ted in Hartsell School.

The family purchased three grave plots in Union Cemetery; after moving to their new home, they had Gerldine's little body exhumed and reburied in Union Cemetery. This graveyard is now called West Concord Cemetery.

That same year Gene Verble left the Atlanta Crackers to play for the Washington Senators. Gene was known as the best glove in the South. There were many professional ballplayers who came out of the local textile leagues, but there were only two baseball players who attended Hartsell School who made it to the Majors: Richard Mauney and Gene Verble.

Gene bought a convenience store at the corner of Wilshire Drive and the Old Charlotte Highway, known then as the Jackson Park Grill, later renamed Gene's Short Stop.

Several years ago, when I was conducting an interview with Gene, he said, "Yes, I made the Majors, but there were many ballplayers that played in the textile league that was better than I was, and your father was one of them."

Chapter 23

Roberta and the Big Three

When they described my birth, they told me it happened in one of the rooms at the Cabarrus Memorial Hospital around eleven thirty, Friday morning, January 15, 1954. Uncle Will and Aunt Nanny were present when the nurse carried me out of the delivery room to show me off. Aunt Nanny said, "You were kicking so hard, you kicked one of the nurse's buttons off her blouse."

Maybe this was a sign of things yet to come; however, I happened to be the first Whittington from our family born in a hospital. All the previous births were delivered at home.

I didn't find out until about five years later how I was named, but after I did, I was kind of confused. While enrolling for the first grade at Hartsell School, they discovered that I had two birth certificates, one stating that I was Harold William Whittington and the other, William Harold Whittington.

When this was discovered, I asked Mom, "What in the world is going on?"

And she explained, "Your uncle, Will, approached your daddy and me and requested that I be named after him."

Will and Nanny were childless. Uncle Will also promised he would buy a new crib for me if I was named in his honor.

Evidently, I surprised everybody at the hospital when I sprung out of the womb, especially Uncle Will, who had not purchased the crib by this time. This pissed my parents off to the point they named me Harold William or William Harold.

Either way, Mom's explanation didn't make much sense. I think Mom told the people at the hospital I was William Harold, and Pappy told them I was Harold William, but it was finally decided that my official name was William Harold before I started school at Hartsell.

How a person gets named is almost as important as the name itself, and I am proud that I was named William after both grandfathers. However, everybody called me Harold. My middle name was chosen after Pappy told Harold Furr I was going to be named after him. Harold Furr happened to be playing baseball with Pappy on the Roberta team at the time. Harold Furr is a fine man, and they called him the Bull because he was rawboned and strong as an ox.

I came into this world a few months before the photo of Shad Whittington, Harold Furr, and Vernon Ford, called the Big Three, was taken, standing there in their old-styled baggy Roberta baseball uniforms. Vernon's middle name happened to be Harold, and Vernon's father was named Harold as well. After I found out how my middle name was chosen, I felt that I rated right up there with the monarchs in Europe. This is why the picture of the Big Three is so dear to me.

Earlier memories include watching Pappy, Vernon Ford, and Richard Mauney play peggy at the edge of Union Cemetery, when I was just a toddler. Richard and Vernon were Pappy's closest friends. By the time I came along, Richard was living in Albermarle, and Vernon was living in a mill house at 66 Robinson Street on the Franklin Mill Hill.

I remember during one visit to Vernon's, Pappy and Vernon were talking on Vernon's front porch, and I was roving around in the yard. I could barely walk at the time, and somehow I ended up between Vernon's and his neighbor's car shed, where I saw a metal stake with this chain attached to it. When I stepped over the chain, it straightened and came off the ground a few inches, and I tripped over it. Before I could get back up, I looked down the length of the chain and saw this large ram connected to the other end. The ram was not pleased with what I did because I had just interrupted his grazing habits. He turned, looked at me, and started to charge; then all at once, out of nowhere, Vernon grabbed the ram by the horns, and Pappy grabbed me up and asked, "What's wrong with you, boy?"

You can never tell what you might run in to, or what might run in to you in people's backyards.

During another visit several years later, Johnson Strube was showing off his prized rooster in Vernon's yard. Johnson lived catty-cornered across the street from Vernon. The rooster, all proud and aggressive, was standing on this sawhorse, and when I walked by, evidently, I got too close, and the rooster jumped on my chest and started flogging me. Johnson rushed over and grabbed the rooster off me, but by this time, it was too late, I had already wet my pants. Everybody in the yard started laughing, but I didn't think it was so funny. I was convinced that the animals on the Franklin Mill Hill were quite dangerous, and Vernon happened to be living in the same mill house where Grandpa Whittington shot the dog on the front porch for biting Uncle Will back in 1920.

Despite this turmoil, I thoroughly enjoyed my visits to Vernon's house. As previously mentioned, Vernon had more nicknames than anybody else. We called him Uncle Bubby, and his wife was known as Aunt Polly, even though we were not related. Vernon's daughter Diane was slightly older than me, whom we called Dicey.

Uncle Bubby was a champion among the children; they flocked to him as if he was the Pied Piper, and I was no exception. To me, he was like a big Santa Claus, and when he picked me up. I could see far off in the distance as if I was standing on top of Mount Mitchell or Grandfather Mountain.

If you were a young boy, as soon as you walked in through the front door, you could not help but notice the assorted array of slingshot prongs displayed on his living room mantle. Uncle Bubby would take me out in the front yard and let me shoot each one.

The only drawback during those visits was Bubby had a jealous and possessive Chihuahua. This dog was black; his eyes were bugged out, he was extremely nervous and shook most of the time, especially if I was nearby. I felt sorry for the dog because I thought he was cold and needed a warm hug, but when I would reach over to pick him up, the dog would bite the blood out of my fingers. Whenever I tried to sit beside Uncle Bubby on his favorite couch; if the dog was nearby, he would jump over Vernon and tear into me.

I determined that the dog was possessed or psychotic because he would act so friendly toward me then all at once turn into a miniature *T.rex*. Our feelings toward each other were mutual; we thoroughly despised each other. If Vernon's dog was around today, I am sure the vet would diagnose the dog as being bipolar.

Even though Vernon was likable and kindhearted, he could be mischievous at times. During the wee hours on some mornings, Vernon would slip out in the yard and shoot his 1903 A3 Springfield Rifle into the water tower on the other side of the Old Charlotte Highway. In no time at all, water would jet out from the bullet hole because Vernon used military ball ammunition that could easily penetrate one side of the tower.

After the water district found out, they had to drain the water tower below the bullet hole and had metal patch welded in place to stop the leak, and this happened several times. Although Vernon was never caught, the authorities sent verbal warnings throughout the mill hill that if it ever happened again, the perpetrator would be caught and severely punished, whereas most everybody knew who the shooter was all along.

The most celebrated story told about Vernon Ford was an incident that took place in 1959, near the end of Union Cemetery Road, where Ben Mynatt Chevrolet is located today. Back then, the lot was vacant, and a traveling caravan would erect tents every summer that contained various FAA displays and other agricultural novelties, but the main attraction that was held included a caged-off area, where the man was supposed to battle the monkey. If the challenger won, he would be awarded $25. This seemed fair enough until Vernon Ford, Norman and Richard Lefler showed up.

Richard, Hulan Lefler's son, had just finished the eighth grade at Hartsell that summer. Norman, Richard's uncle, was one of the few Leflers who did not play baseball. Richard said, "Uncle Norman looked a lot like the actor Strother Martin."

Norman and Vernon had been drinking that evening and felt they could defeat the monkey and claim the prize.

Norman was the first to accept the challenge. Before Norman stepped into the cage, he was fitted with a football helmet and a catcher's chest protector. Just before the animal trainer/caretaker opened the cage door, he gave Norman some last-minute advice. He said, "Now you can do what you won't to do, but this animal will be as rough with you as you are to him."

When Norman entered the ring, he realized he wasn't facing a monkey; monkeys have tails and hang out in trees. This was a full-grown male chimpanzee, and chimpanzees have five times the strength of a human.

Norman charged the chimp, but the chimp just sidestepped him and backhanded Norman so hard, he went crashing into the bars, and was immediately on top of Norman. Norman never had a chance. After that, the animal trainer and an assistant rushed in; the trainer went in to distract the chimp, while the assistant pulled Norman out of the cage. As soon as Norman was out of the cage, he started shedding his protective gear and was pleading, "Get him, Uncle Vernon, get him."

Vernon suited up as quickly as he could, and when he entered the ring, even before the cage door slammed behind him, he hit the chimpanzee right between the eyes with a straight right hand. This sent the chimp into a frenzy. The chimp climbed to the top of the cage, went round and round; all the while, he was making loud agitated chimp noises. Then all at once, the chimp sprang from the top of the cage and landed on Vernon. The full force was concentrated on Vernon's left shoulder, which drove him to the ground and broke his collarbone. The animal grabbed Vernon by the helmet and started slamming him into the side of the cage. It took additional help to get Vernon out of the cage without receiving further injuries.

Norman and Richard helped Vernon get to the car, and Norman drove him to the Cabarrus Memorial Hospital, where Vernon was admitted. Richard said, "As soon as they got to the hospital, the staff took Vernon into one of the rooms, while Norman and I were waiting at the front desk."

The hospital receptionist, who had to fill out the necessary paperwork, asked Norman, "How did your friend get hurt?"

Norman answered, "Ma'am, he was fightin' a gorilla."

She asked, "What did you say?"

Norman answered again, "I told you he was fightin' a gorilla."

FENCEBUSTERS – look forward to Thursday night when Concord's newly formed semi-pro team makes its debut against Rockwell at Webb Field.

This formidable trio has proved in the past their ability to rattle the planks on outfield walls.

Other teams in the Granite Belt League opening Thursday night are Kannapolis at Landis and Spencer at China Grove.

(Tribune Staff Photo)

Shad and Vernon were almost inseparable and were seen together in most of the baseball photos, especially during the start up of a newly formed team called Concord Patriots, which was scheduled to play within the Granite Belt League. A younger group of ballplayers started to emerge, namely Red McClamrock, Bernie Edwards, Richard Lapish, Frank and Harold Mauney, to name a few.

Richard Lapish recalled, "It was good to play ball with Shad and George because we would be kind of nervous, but Shad and George would tell so many funny stories, it would put us at ease."

The younger players would always get a kick out of asking Shad if this batter or that one could hit; if the person they asked about was a good hitter, Shad would say, "He can knock a ball nine miles out of the ballpark," but if the hitter they inquired about was not very good, Shad would tell them, "That guy couldn't hit Kate Smith in the ass with an ironing board," and the players would fall over laughing.

Kate Smith happened to be a very renowned popular singer during Pap's time frame, but she was also quite large.

Richard also stated, "The Concord Patriots was a crackerjack team, and we won everything that year. The Patriots roster was a mixture of semipro, former professional, and college baseball players. Johnnie Pair was the manager, Johnny Clark played left field, Vernon Ford in center, and Buddy Klutz was in right field. Bub Deaton played third, Beetle Autin was the shortstop, and Hal Washam played second. Shad and Cliff Evans would alternate playing first base, or Shad would catch if I was scheduled to pitch. Our pitchers were Big George Hatley, Larry (Satch) Sedberry, Gerald Blackburn, and I pitched in that rotation as well."

Regardless of Shad's age, he was still a dominant hitter, and the pitchers appearing on the scene had to apply additional pressure just to get him out. Richard Lapish also told me, "While we were playing in China Grove one night, a right-handed pitcher named Fred Motley hit Shad with a wild pitch just a couple of inches above his right ear. It was a glancing blow-the ball bounced off his head and went over the back stop." The back stop was not equipped with a wire overhang like most other backstops, and this event happened seven years before batting helmets were used. "Shad was very wobbly and weak-kneed as he started walking toward first base."

Shad said, "One leg wanted to go one way and the other leg tried to go another."

Shad's teammates could see blood trickling down the side of his face, ran over to him, and asked, "Shad, are you all right?"

Shad looked at his concerned team members and said, "Hell, that pitcher couldn't bust a damn egg."

I noticed that members of Pappy's generation just had to get away and start fishing, regardless if they caught anything or not. Somehow they found solace at the edge of a river or by fishing in a pond without any ripples. Shad and Vernon spent a lot their time fishing the creeks, rivers, and ponds together. Every spring, when the male cardinals began to sing and the dogwoods started to bloom, they would head down to Santee Cooper, South Carolina, to fish for crappies.

A summer ritual since the end of WW2 commenced when the mills closed for summer vacation, and they would drive over to Carolina Beach, where Pappy, Vernon, Howard, and Millie Hooks would rent a beach house for the week and go out deep-sea fishing for red and silver snappers.

When Shad and Vernon weren't playing ball or umpiring on Friday evenings or on Saturdays, they would invite Johnson Strube and Eddie Kennedy to hunt hawks in the country. They had quite an array of varmint rifles, such as .22 Hornets, the .22-250, and the notorious .220 Swift, complete with a ten-power mounted scope. The farmers welcomed the hawk hunters because those chicken hawks would kill a lot of their chickens.

Vernon marveled at Shad's ability with a rifle, and most everybody around would take their rifles to Shad to zero and maybe teach them how to shoot top dead center. Pappy's repeat customer was Doc Sapp, a Concord physician, who paid Shad dearly to set up his big game rifles before Doc went to Africa to hunt rhino.

Vernon and Pappy would go squirrel-hunting at Uncle Cliff's in Stanly County, along Stoney Run Creek, or they might hunt in the woods behind our house. In the late fall and winter, they hunted for rabbits and quail (bobwhites) in the surrounding fields and pastures. It was easy to determine that Vernon Ford was Pappy's closest friend.

Chapter 24

The Weekend Warrior

Mama treated Pappy like he was the king of Siam. I remember there were evenings when Mom would pour warm water into a pan and then sprinkle Epsom salt into the water so Pappy could soak his feet. She would clip his calloused nails and wash his feet just before he went to work, like something out of the Bible. In all those years, Mom never learned to drive a car, so she had to rely on Pappy or others to give her a ride.

Mom fixed us good meals. Through the week, breakfast consisted of sausage patties or bacon with scrambled eggs, grits, and biscuits that came out of a can. Pappy liked his eggs over easy or sunny side up. The meal was usually topped off with a glass of white milk; Pappy called it sweet milk, something other than buttermilk.

On some mornings, we ate liver mush instead of sausage or bacon. The Sunday breakfast was special, with eggs, grits, and fried pork chops. Mom made homemade biscuits on Sunday. I remember an occasion where one of Pappy's friends had killed a black bear in the mountains. We had bear sausage, and it was very good.

The evening meal or supper was fresh vegetables from our garden or from the canned vegetables Mom had stored on our back porch and some type of soft meat. Pappy would say, "Give me some of them maters and taters," tomatoes and potatoes. Mama and Pappy had false teeth and could not eat tough meat.

We never ate sweets before the meal, desserts came after, and Mom always had a cake or maybe an apple or cherry pie ready. It was always a treat to see Mom make a cake because my sister Eva and I got to lick either the spoon or the beaters from the mixer that was heavily laden with chocolate. After lunch, Pappy would let us eat some of his Little Debbie cakes he had stored in one of the kitchen cabinets or on top the refrigerator.

Mom did our grocery-shopping at the Fleetwood Shopping Center, later named the Stop & Shop, on Union Cemetery Road where old Coley Airport used to be. Sometimes she would send me to purchase stuff at Stallings Grocery on the corner of Highland Avenue and Poplar Street.

It was not all peaches and cream in this boy land because there were disturbing times that spanned from the time I was a first-grader at Hartsell School until I was a freshman in high school.

A weekend warrior is commonly known that describes a military person serving in the National Guard or the military reserve. Brother Ted called Pappy a weekend warrior because of the way he conducted himself during his weekend drinking sprees. Pappy did not drink through the week, he only drank during the weekends, so the weekend maelstroms were very prominent throughout the 1960s.

Pappy did not drink very often during the spring and summer months because he was involved with umpiring baseball or softball. But when the season was over, we knew we were in for quite a surprise about every weekend.

Those who worked the third shift worked Sunday through Thursday nights, and they had Friday and Saturday nights off. Mama and I would hold our breath when Friday evening rolled around. We paid close attention to where Pappy went to purchase his weekend refreshments.

If he chose to drive to the county line and pick up beer, we would give a sigh of relief, Cabarrus County was a dry county at the time, but if he drove to the ABC store to buy a fifth of Carstairs or a bottle of Canadian Club or Southern Comfort, we knew that our weekend would be hell on earth. Pappy didn't drink the hard stuff straight; he mixed his drinks with Sun Drop.

We usually had a fish fry at our house every Friday or Saturday night, and if others came over, such as Vernon and Polly Ford, or Richard and Rachael Mauney, or Brother Ted and Carolyn, the threat of an explosion would be lessened. However, if it was just Mom and I there and hard liquor was consumed, we would bear the brunt of whatever development that might lie ahead.

Pap's personality change was similar to the story of Jekyll and Hyde, but this transformation took place right before our eyes. I have never seen anyone else display a more abrupt change in behavior than Pappy did. To me, he was a Superman, but whisky and hard liquor was his kryptonite.

After dinner, he would start cussing and raising hell, so we would slip off into our bedrooms and pretend we were asleep, but it didn't matter. The cussing, ranting, and raving would not stop, whether someone was with him or he was alone. He acted as if he were plagued by some inscrutable inner crucifixion.

We would wait until after about thirty minutes of silence, then Mom and I would ease back into the kitchen, where we would find him either passed out on the floor or with his head down on the kitchen table fast asleep. Mom and I would struggle carrying him into the bedroom in a way so we would not wake the sleeping dragon. This was usually the way most weekends went, but there were times that were much worse.

One night I stayed up with Pappy during one of those episodes. Pappy started talking about women, and then I heard Mom shout from the bedroom, reminding Pappy that I was not of age to hear that kind of talk. Surprisingly enough, he changed the subject.

A few moments later, I noticed that Pappy was about to make a serious mistake. Pappy had just eaten a mess of fish, and he was opening the refrigerator to pour himself a glass of milk. I knew that he was allergic to any fish and milk combination. I didn't know why he didn't remember that, so I said, "Pap, you are not supposed to eat fish and drink milk," and he said, "Boy, you don't know what the hell you are talking about."

He got very sick and vomited most of the night. The next day, after he was sober, he told me how bad he felt. Then I told him that I tried to warn him the night before. He looked at me, laughed, and said, "I must have been a damned nitwit."

That was the only time I have ever heard him call himself a nitwit. Pappy used the term *nitwit* to describe other people more than any of the other Three Stooges' quotes.

There were many episodes like those throughout the years that were considered minor in nature, like small earthquakes or tremors. But the first major quake happened when I was in the first grade at Hartsell School.

On December 24, 1960, Christmas Eve, we had just returned from Grandpa and Grandma Goodman's. Every year they would have all the relatives come up and exchange gifts. It was like having two Christmases, but we could open our presents before we left Grandma's. Grandpa had given me a brand new pocketknife. I was happier than ever because whenever we went to Grandpa's, it was quite a celebration. I didn't know there was that much food and candy in the world. However, on the way back to Concord, hardly any words were spoken between Pap and Mom. I knew there was something that was said or something was done that had set Pappy off.

I think Mom was in the early stage of pregnancy with Eva, and I am uncertain if anyone knew this at the time. As soon as we came in through the back door and made it to the living room, Pappy grabbed Mama and threw her down on the floor. Mom told me what happened next because I couldn't remember. She said I stood over her, opened my new pocketknife, pointed it at Pap, and with a trembling hand, said, "Don't you touch my mama again."

Mom went on to say, "Your daddy froze and turned white as a sheet then left the room."

We didn't have a phone at the time, so we couldn't call anyone for help. After Pappy went to sleep, we slipped out of the house, woke a neighbor, and that neighbor called a cab that took us back to Grandpa's place in China Grove. Could you could imagine how much that cab bill was for that twenty-two-mile trip on a mill worker's salary?

The separation lasted about a week, and during that time, Shad made several visits to Mom's mill gate to ask for forgiveness. Mama finally relented, and we returned home.

The lives of certain ballplayers were just as rough off the field as they were on the field, and what follows is another example to prove that statement. Johnson Strube and Pappy went hawk-hunting one Saturday all day. They had been drinking all day as well, and their hunt ended after they stopped off at a beer hall. Pappy called beer halls jip joints. One thing led to another, and before long, a fight broke out behind the beer joint between Pappy and one of four men in the opposing group. Johnson said, "Shad was so drunk. He was missing with his punches, and the other guy was tearing Shad's head up. Both of Shad's eyes were covered in blood, and then Shad connected with a left hook that knocked the guy up against a tree, but the blow also knocked the guy's front teeth out."

Things went bad in a hurry. The other three guys tried to jump in, but Johnson fired a warning shot right past one guy's head then stated, "I will kill all three of you with the next three shots."

The three men ran off into the woods, then Johnson put the rifle down and picked up a big rock, ran over to the guy Pappy had knocked out, and said, "Shad, let me cave his head in with this rock."

Pappy stopped Johnson from killing the guy. Pappy and Johnson drove away in Pap's car and left the unconscious fellow lying beside the tree.

About an hour later, Pappy told Johnson he wasn't through kicking the man's ass, so they drove back to the scene only to find the man gone. Pappy knew where the guy lived and went to his house for a second round. The guy's wife was shocked after she answered the door and saw Pappy standing out on the front porch, along with Johnson who was holding the .220 Swift Rifle at port arms. Pappy asked her, "Where is your husband?"

And she answered, "He is not doing so well, somebody knocked his front teeth out."

Then Pappy said, "I am the one that knocked his teeth out," then Pappy and Johnson left.

This reminded me of something Pappy used to say at the breakfast table. He would hold up his left arm, make a fist, then say, "This is six months in the hospital." Then he raised his right hand, shook his fist, then said, "And this is sudden death."

During the summer of '66, I was scheduled to go stay with Uncle Cliff and Aunt Laurie's in Stanly County for two weeks. I was really looking forward to my visit because this place was way out in the country, and it was a boyhood utopia.

Pappy was supposed to drive me down to Uncle Cliff's, but he wanted to take Mom and Eva along. The problem was Pappy had been drinking the hard stuff all day, and Mom knew he normally drove like a race car driver when he was sober, but while he was drinking, he drove even worse. Pappy started raising hell and ordered everybody to get in the car, so we piled in the '54 blue Ford Station Wagon, and the treacherous journey began.

On the way down, Pappy almost wrecked a couple of times, and Mom started yelling, "Jim, stop the car and let us out!"

Pap just ignored her, then Mom grabbed the steering wheel, and Pappy backhanded her in the face. Mom recovered and slapped him back. They slapped each other, back and forth, which seemed to take forever, and the entire time, we were traveling at least seventy miles per hour along Highway 200, a winding country road. While this front-seat battle was taking place, I reached into the back of the Station Wagon and started loading my .22 rifle. Mom saw what I was doing and while she was being hit, said, "No, Harold, no."

Then Pappy stopped the car, and Mom, my sister Eva and I jumped out and started walking up the road.

Pappy got out, ran over to Eva, grabbed her up, and put her back into the car. We had no other choice but to get back inside as well. At this point, Pappy turned the car around and headed back home. The summer vacation that I was looking forward to suddenly turned into a tragedy.

After we got back home, that night seemed to be one of the longest nights I could remember. We kept our clothes on when we went to bed and acted like we were asleep. I had two twelve-gauge shotgun shells in my hand tucked out of sight underneath my pillow.

Mom waited until Pappy passed out in the kitchen, then she quietly rousted us up. We packed a few clothes and slipped out of the house. As we were walking down Linden Avenue, I told Mom that we should go over to the house of my friend Terry Gledhill for help.

When Mom knocked on the door, a surprised Bob Gledhill, Terry's father, answered and listened to Mom's story. Bob drove us over to Grandma's place, and we stayed in Rowan County for at least two weeks. I didn't know what was going to happen next or if we would ever return. During our two-week stay, there were the obligatory visits from Pappy at Mom's mill gate. Only this time she held firm. She wanted real change, followed by a solemn promise that it would never happen again.

When Mama decided to return home, nobody in the Goodman family wanted her to go. Just before we started to leave, Grandpa told Mom, "I told you not to go back to him the last time, and this time you are on your own—don't come back."

Grandpa and Mama were crying as we walked out through the Goodman front door. Shad continued to drink, but the violent fights and outbursts toward Mom ceased.

I would hope that no one would have to endure the lifestyle I described. I knew other fathers who were much worse than mine. The drunk, in his inebriated state, can cause mental and physical damage to the sober ones around and not even remember it the next day. Life is hard enough without having to deal with this self-imposed anguish and stress.

Just before I started high school, Pappy traded in his '64 Station Wagon for a 1968 Ford Ranger pickup truck. This was the vehicle I drove while I was learning to drive. As previously mentioned, Pappy owned only Ford products, and his vehicles were three-speed standard transmissions with the gearshift on the column.

One day, while he was letting me drive this truck out to my high school, he wanted me to pull over to the side of Zion Church Road. He stepped out of the truck and just stared out across the field. I shut the truck off and walked over beside him, and he pointed to a cow pasture just beside the railroad track of the Franklin Mill and said, "This is where we used to play."

He was pointing to what used to be the Franklin Mill Baseball Field, which had vanished from the American scene thirty-one years ago. I thought about what had occurred many times up through the years, and I wish I could have seen through his eyes what he was reminiscing for that brief moment.

During the winter of 1968, an event took place that will remain etched in my memory. It involved my father and another ballplayer he previously played with, whose name I will not mention.

Pappy and this fellow were drinking heavily, and I can remember there had been a blanket of snow that had fallen previously that day. Mom and Eva were visiting with another family, and it was just those two and me at the house. They were already quite soused before I left to go visit Terry Gledhill.

Terry and I would watch the bullfights over at his house on Friday nights. We didn't understand why there was so much to do about killing a bull. We wanted to see the bull tear into the matador. After the bullfights were over, I returned home just to find the two ballplayers were still enjoying their drunken social event, but what happened next turned out to be just as bloody as the bullfights that I had been watching.

As the night drew on, the ballplayers were exchanging words in the kitchen, and then it happened. A comment was made that was intended to be a joke, which was taken out of context, and the fight started. I saw firsthand what I had only heard about through others as to Pappy's speed, power, and viciousness.

The fight started in the kitchen and traversed through the living room and the bedroom. There were times when I tried to intervene, only to be in the way. I was shocked when our guest pulled out a .32 Cobra Colt pistol and hit Pappy in the head three times in a row. Besides opening a gash in my father's head, it just made Pappy more determined to eliminate his opponent that much more.

It must be noted that Pap's opponent was twenty years younger and should have had the advantage, but reality proved otherwise. I noticed that the faces of both fighters were covered in blood. They looked like Indians wearing war paint, and by this time, Shad's opponent was suffering from a broken nose and two broken ribs. There was also blood on the walls, the furniture, and all over my white T-shirt as well.

There was a short lull during the fight, while both paused to catch their breath, and I knew it was going to escalate. Pappy said, "I've had enough of you."

I looked at Pappy's opponent and said, "You need to get out of here because he is going to kill you."

Pappy reached up over the bedroom door and took down his double-barreled twelve-gauge shotgun, and I knew it was loaded with number 6 shot in the right-hand barrel, and the left barrel had a number 4 shotgun shell ready. This load was normally for rabbits and squirrels, but at close range, the weapon would make mincemeat out of a human.

I rushed toward Pappy and grabbed the barrel of the shotgun, pleading for Pappy not to shoot him. This time my request was heard, and he relinquished the gun, and by this time, I was in possession of the pistol and the shotgun.

There was another pause, and both men were standing around the kerosene heater in the living room. Pappy took out his Cannon Mill terry cloth rag he kept in his back pocket and started wiping the blood off his face, and for the strangest reason, Pap's opponent asked if he could use the rag to wipe his face. Pappy looked at the guy, balled the rag up, said, "Here," and hit him in the face with the rag. His opponent picked up the rag, started wiping the blood off his face, handed the rag back, and said, "Thank you, Shad."

Not long after that, they loaded into the truck, and Pappy drove him home. I must admit that was one hell of a night.

Chapter 25

And Along Came Eva

Mom gave birth to my sister Eva Marlene on October 16, 1960, and it was quite a jubilee. Eva was named after our Grandmother Whittington. My sister was always a puzzle to me. She was different from anything I had ever witnessed. She carried her favorite baby doll Suzy around at all times. Eva did not use a pacifier; she sucked her thumb but only if she had a Cannon Mill terry cloth rag in her hand. She would, could tickle her upper lip with the corner of the rag in the process.

Eva could cry longer and louder than any other human on earth or any animal that I had seen on Mutual of Omaha's *Wild Kingdom*. I would ask Mom, "How can she cry like that without even taking a breath?"

Later in life, she became a wonderful gospel singer, and I know how she achieved such superb voice and breath control; it was through crying.

The most memorable thought I had about my sister happened in our living room. I remember kneeling beside the rocking chair when I saw Eva, who was wearing diapers and a little red dress, pull her little body off the floor using the corner of the couch. With wobbly legs, she took her first steps across the room right into my arms. Although she was too young to remember, I will never forget that moment. This is a significant point that will be visited later in this story.

As Eva and I grew older, we would have rag fights. We threw those same type terry cloth rags they made at the mill at each other after we tied a couple of knots in the rags so they could fly straight. Sometimes we would wet those rags so they would seem to stick to whatever they hit.

I had the advantage because I was older, and I had been pitching for the Hartsell Bulldogs for several seasons. Man, it was good to have a younger sister because she was a live moving target, and it was quite entertaining when the rag would appear to stick to Eva's face after I hit the mark.

This feeling of utopia was short-lived because after Mom came home from work, Eva would tell her how mean I was, and I would end up getting spanked. Mom did the spanking in the family. Pappy didn't have to. All he had to do was raise his voice or start taking off his belt, and the illicit behavior would cease.

The stated comment heard throughout the family was that Eva was the first female born in the Whittington family in over one-hundred years, which I found out later was not true. Eva was the first girl born in the family that lived. I discovered that I had an elder sister by accident.

When I was about twelve, I happened to be squirrel-hunting behind the house one afternoon, just beside Union Cemetery. I was walking around a den tree when I noticed a little grave marker beneath the tree. The name on the marker was Gerldine Whittington. I lost interest in the squirrel that I was after and went straight home. I told Mama about the grave, and she told me I had an elder sister who did not survive. I was shocked, and I believe had I not stumbled upon that grave, I would never have known that I had an elder sister. It was as if her memory had been wiped clean from some invisible slate.

Chapter 26

Uncle Clarence

In late fall of 1959, Pappy took me up to Uncle Clarence's to go squirrel-hunting. I was five years old at the time. On the way up, Pappy said that I had better behave while I was up there because if I didn't, Aunt Beulah, Clarence's wife, a Cherokee Indian woman, would just take me out back and scalp me, and there is nothing anybody could do to stop her. His words shook me up quite a bit.

We arrived just before the sun came up, and I noticed that the last five miles of the trip were dirt roads. When we got out of the vehicle, I could see that the house was lit by oil lamps, instead of electricity, and as we came inside, I noticed there was no radio or TV. I walked into the kitchen and saw Aunt Beulah putting wood into her metal stove, the same type stove Aunt Laurie had down in Stanly County. It amazed me the way Aunt Beulah used this piece of metal to hook under the round burners and lift them before she put the wood inside.

I also noticed that four places had been set at the table, but the plates were upside down. When breakfast was ready, she called us into the kitchen and before she served the food, she flipped the plates over and took a cloth and wiped each plate then served a breakfast fit for kings. I felt brave at that moment and asked, "Aunt Beulah, why do you flip the plates upside down?"

And she answered, "I don't want soot to get on my plates."

Somehow I made it through breakfast without getting scalped.

After breakfast, Pappy and I went out the back door and walked down the steps and started loading our .22-caliber rifles. While we were doing so, I saw chickens flying down from the tree limbs, where they had been roosting the night before, and realized where our fresh eggs for breakfast came.

I was hunting with a Winchester semiautomatic rifle, and Pappy had his Model 75 Winchester, the same type rifle he took target-practice with when he was in the navy, complete with a shoulder strap and a six-power Junior Unertl Scope. We crossed a logging trail just behind the house and settled into a thick grove of pine trees.

Pappy sat down by a big pine tree, and he pointed to a tree nearby, where I was supposed to sit. Pappy called this still-hunting, where you would sit quietly and wait for the squirrels to come out. He told me to sit off to his right where he could see me. It was cold that morning, and I could see my breath whenever I exhaled, and I wondered if the squirrels could see it too. I noticed that Pappy picked a spot where we would not be looking into the rising sun when we shot.

Soon afterward, I saw Pappy raise his rifle to his shoulder, but he didn't shoot. He spotted a squirrel in the top of a very tall pine tree and could have made the shot at any time, but it was important to him that I take the shot. He motioned me over to sit by him. I eased into position, it took me a little while to find the squirrel, then I took aim, using fine sight, and squeezed the trigger; the same way I was taught to shoot small rocks or the bottoms of spent shotgun shells in the backyard at home. Then I fired, but the squirrel didn't fall, so I fired again, and Pappy said, "Boy, you have already killed the squirrel, just give him a chance to fall out of the tree."

His eyesight was exceptional even at this stage in his life. He came from a time when bullets were not so plentiful, so extra shots were just a waste of ammunition.

A few seconds later, the squirrel fell out of the tree, but we did not go over to where the squirrel fell right away because there were other squirrels out, and he didn't want to scare them off. Although Pappy didn't say much, I could tell that he was proud of my shot, that somehow I had completed an ancient rite of passage that morning, a ceremony that was as old as the hills where we were hunting.

When we crossed the logging trail on the way back to the house, I was carrying six squirrels by the tail because Pap shot five other squirrels before he decided to gather our game. It is very important to remember where every squirrel fell when you still hunt.

When we stepped out on the logging trail, Uncle Clarence came out of the pines the same time we did. He was not carrying a gun, and evidently, he had been with us the entire time, but I never saw or heard him.

Before we went inside, I handed the squirrels to Aunt Beulah, and Uncle Clarence stopped by the mule pen and started talking to his mule Frank, just as if he was talking to a person, and I think the mule could understand what he said. I saw Uncle Cliff, Clarence, and Pappy's half-brother talk to his mules the same way in Stanly County.

After I unloaded my rifle, Uncle Clarence said to me in his booming voice, "Boy, go down to the spring and draw some water."

So I grabbed a bucket and crossed over Route 5 to get the water. When I got to the mouth of this shallow well, the water was cold and clear because this was an opening of an underground mountain stream. I saw this ladle hanging on a limb of a small tree nearby, so I started filling the bucket with water. The water was so clear I could see a large crawdad on the sandy bottom, and he didn't move the entire time I ladled the water from the stream.

On the way up to the house, I saw the horseshoe pits and noticed just beside one of the pits, where Uncle Clarence had a set of horseshoes and a set of mule shoes hanging on the limb of a cedar tree.

Much to my surprise, after I returned with the water, Pappy had gone out and cut the prongs from a dogwood tree he had spotted earlier, and he took those prongs home and crafted them into my first adult-sized slingshot. Oh, I had those kiddy slingshots they sell at the store, but they were just bean flips. This slingshot was the real McCoy, like moving up to the Major Leagues in the slingshot world. Where Pappy was concerned, as soon as you passed one test, you can be assured that another one would follow.

Around six years after that hunting trip, Pappy came into my bedroom to wake me one morning and said in a low voice, "Your Uncle Clarence died this morning."

I remained motionless in bed for a while and reminisced about the visits we made to his place and all the stories I had heard about him.

Uncle Clarence died on December 27, 1965. He was sixty-two years old. We went to his funeral near Lincolton. I remember watching Aunt Beulah during the ceremony. She seemed stoic and just stared far off over the horizon as if she were looking for him somewhere out in the distance. The couple never had children, and I wondered what she would do for the rest of her life.

Uncle Clarence was buried between two rows of majestic pine trees, and Brother Ted told Pappy after the ceremony, "They couldn't have buried him in a better place. Do you remember that song he used to sing, 'In the pines, in the pines, where the sun never shines?'

We never visited Lincolton again after Uncle Clarence died, so Aunt Beulah just seemed to vanish into obscurity.

Chapter 27

Slingshots, Horseshoes, and Playing Peggy

By the time Uncle Clarence passed away, I would have had my original slingshot for about six years. I became very proficient and could shoot accurately. Only a few boys of my generation even carried a slingshot, yet almost everyone in the generation before me had slingshots.

I thought I was the best slingshot shooter in the area, perhaps the best in the state, until Pappy walked around to the back of our house, where I was shooting in the backyard. He said, "Let me try out your slingshot."

I handed him my slingshot; he took the prongs, straightened out the rubbers, and picked up three granite stones.

Now all he needed was a target. He saw a solitary clothes pin that Mom had left on the clothesline, and without any practice shots, he shot the clothes pin and broke off one of the wooden arms of the pin. As soon as the clothes pin stopped spinning, he shot again and broke off the other arm. Now there was only the metal clip and half of the clothes pin hanging on the line.

His third shot knocked the rest of the clothes pin out in the garden. He handed the slingshot back to me and said, "That is a pretty good shooting slingshot," and just walked back inside the house.

A slingshot does not have any sights; the shooter has to use instinct and feel. It would have taken me ten to fifteen shots to do what he did in only three. I convinced myself that I was still a good shot, but there was no way I could match his accuracy.

I shot for fun, but those of his generation not only shot for fun, but they also used their slingshots as a hunting tool. When Pappy was my age, if he missed, his family might not have fresh meat that day. There were times when it wasn't easy to realize that you are the son of a superman.

His precision and accuracy not only included shooting. Just on the other side of the clothesline were two horseshoe pits, and from early spring to late fall, we would pitch horseshoes almost every day. There were many times when I would be out back pitching horseshoes alone, and Pappy would step out back and ask, "Do you want to pitch a few?"

And of course, I would accept the challenge.

When he pitched, he turned his shoes once, and his pitches hit flat and would slide ever so nicely around the stake. Furthermore, he didn't have to warm up like I did; as soon as he threw his first pitch, he was on target. If I didn't throw a ringer at least 50 percent of the time, I would not stand a chance.

We kept score differently than in a regulation horseshoe game. The closest shoe to the stake was equal to a point. A leaner was three points, and a ringer equaled five points. If two individuals were playing, the first player to reach eleven points won, and if teams played, twenty-one points was the winning score. Our games would be over in no time at all with this scoring system.

After Pappy slaughtered me three games in a row, he said, "Well, I believe I'll go back in the house."

He did not gloat over his wins, nor was he egotistical when he beat his opponents. He would just look at his opponent and say, "What's wrong, I thought you wanted to pitch horseshoes?"

If he wanted to rub it in, he would switch over and start pitching left-handed. He could out-pitch his opponent with either hand.

Ted and I could sometimes match him, if we warmed up for about thirty minutes to an hour before he showed up. Over the many years of pitching against him, we only won a small percentage of games. I never knew anyone who could consistently beat my father pitching horseshoes. He could have made a living at the game had he wanted to.

Lowell Ferguson ran a barbershop on the Roberta Road, beside Zeb Kennedy's Pond, just across the street from the Jackson Park housing area. Pappy would take me over to Lowell's place to get my haircuts from time to time. Like many others in the area, Lowell had horseshoe pits at his house, and he considered himself an accomplished player. Lowell also happened to have a talking myna bird in his shop, and the bird could talk up a storm.

While I was getting my haircut, Lowell challenged Pappy in horseshoes, and Pappy said, "Well, you know where I live, come on by anytime." As we were leaving Lowell's shop, Pappy said, "I don't know who talks the most, Lowell or that damn bird."

One Friday evening, not too long after the haircut, Brother Ted, his wife Carolyn, and Nick Furr came over to eat some fish. While the fish were frying, we went out back to celebrate a family ritual and started pitching horseshoes.

While we were playing, we saw four people walking toward us across a big plowed field. We could hear one member in the group, shouting out challenges, which we gladly accepted. The challenger happened to be Lowell Ferguson, and he had three other guys with him. I was excited because I really wanted to know what it would be like to pitch horseshoes against normal humans.

No matter how Lowell stacked his teams, we won every game. Nick Furr told one of the players, talking about me, "Man, I would be ashamed if I let a sixth-grader beat me like that." When it was Pappy's turn to pitch against Lowell, he told Lowell, "I am going to cut you some slack," and started pitching left-handed.

Lowell never had a chance, which frustrated Lowell to the point of no return.

Lowell gathered up his group and said, "Well, Shad, we need to get back to the house."

As the defeated group started their return trip across the field, Ted yelled, "Hey, Lowell, you all come back now, you hear, and make sure you tell your bird how you beat the Whittingtons today!"

After the games were over; we settled down and enjoyed a well-prepared mess of fish. Ted gave his famous laugh and asked, "What do you think about that, Pap?"

And Pappy said, "We made Lowell and his bunch look like Ned in the *First Reader*." All of us started laughing when Pappy added, "Lowell's talking bird makes more sense than he does."

The word of Lowell's defeat traveled as fast as the speed of sound throughout the community, so Lowell never came back. That particular day happened to be one of the better days I spent while growing up.

Our garden was just behind those horseshoe pits, and about thirty yards from the southwest corner of our garden was Zeb Kennedy's dirt racetrack. This racetrack is where Eddie Kennedy would test run his midget racer when he was a youngster. We used to get together and play peggy on the infield of that racetrack every fall.

All that was needed to play was two or more players and three pieces of wood. Those three pieces of wood were called the riser, the peggy, and the peggy stick. Pap was a master peggy player and definitely the game's biggest promoter. Pappy played peggy with his friends while he was growing up on the Franklin Mill Hill.

We cut our peggys and peggy sticks from dogwood trees because those trees grew straight, and the wood was tough and durable. Others preferred to use hickory; however, the type of wood used was entirely up to the individual player. This game was unique because you could not buy your equipment from a local sporting goods store; you had to make your equipment from scratch, compliments of Mother Nature.

The preparation for the game was an adventure in itself that required a trip to the woods, equipped with a handsaw and a pocketknife, searching for the trees that were the right size. We spent a lot of time in the woods behind the house, picking blackberries or plums, fishing, and hunting, and by doing so, we knew every creek bed, every briar patch, and where the dogwoods grew. Their white and pink blooms were very prominent in the spring; they grew along fence lines, hedgerows, and at the edge of the woods.

Almost everyone in those days carried a pocketknife. A person would feel incomplete if they left the house without their knife. Most of the people in our area were cotton mill workers, carpenters, or farmers, and having a well-honed knife was an absolute necessity. You could tell a lot about a person judging from the type of knife they carried and how they took care of their knife.

Pappy taught all his children how to sharpen a knife. All the blades on Pappy's knife were extremely sharp, and the hinges were well oiled. Having a dull knife in the Whittington family was sacrilegious, and if we pulled a dull knife out of our pockets around our father, he would have called us a nitwit or an infidel. The knife was a required item when preparing for and playing peggy.

Many of my friends also played peggy. It was considered a boys game, but we let the girls play too. Baseball players loved this game because it promoted hitting, and it helped develop quick wrists; however, football and basketball players and even the nonathletic types enjoyed this game as well.

Over the course of years, there were many who played this game in our area, and they include Shad, Ted, Jeff and Eva Whittington, Willard, Luke, Marvin, Frank, Richard and Harold Mauney, Cliff, Bill, Thurman and Vernon Ford, James, Link, Hughland, also Richard Lefler, Robert Stallings, Terry Gledhill, Tim Hatley, Bobby Canaday, Gene Verble, Allen Honeycutt, die Kennedy, Nick Furr, Junior Ferguson, Richard Lapish, Bill, Howard Hooks Sr. and Jr., Bill, Lanny and Cynthia Edwards, and me or anybody else who happened to be passing through the neighborhood that day.

This list does not include those players who played peggy on the Brown, Norcott, Cabarrus, and Roberta mills areas. Nor does it include the farmers who played in the rural areas of Cabarrus, Stanly, and Union counties. This game was played as far west as Lincolnton during my era.

It would be difficult to say just how popular and widespread this game was in North Carolina prior to father's generation because it was never chronicled. The players passed their stories by word of mouth only, might explain why this ancient game has been lost to history.

It is amazing how such a ridiculously simple little game could harness so much magic and bring so much enjoyment to groups of all ages, yet it has been said that the simple things in life are the ones most cherished. I guarantee that if any of the former peggy players should happen to read this story, I am sure a smile would appear on their faces, their hearts would become warmer, and they would reminisce about a time and place of endearment. Yes, this is the game called peggy.

Many years have passed since I played my first game of peggy, and I am deeply saddened that many of those names mentioned previously are no longer with us. Peggy had its rightful place in history and highlighted a very long era. But I think that our particular version of the game could be attributed to one man, my father, who kept the game alive long after its popularity waned in other regions.

Pappy was one of the few hitters who could switch hit with power; his ability was unmatched. We were amazed by his raw and natural talent, but we knew that during the early '60s, we were seeing the watered-down version of this baseball champion. During which, he would have been at least fifty years old. We could only imagine what he was capable of when he was in his prime.

Pappy rallied and brought out the essence of community, instilled the spirit of competition and camaraderie in all the people around him. He was the Pied Piper of the neighborhood; he could motivate, excite, and reach even the most juvenile or antisocial person, which was just one of his many gifts.

Why, in no time at all, after discussing this game with the youngsters on our front porch, those young players could be seen following him out to the racetrack, like a line of eager ducklings ready to play their newly founded game. If you didn't happen to see this parade, you could almost tell how many players were involved by noticing the piles of wood shavings they left in the yard around the outside of our porch.

If someone would have drawn a sketch or painted a picture of this front-porch procession, they would have been able to capture some of the magic of peggy, as rustic as any Norman Rockwell painting.

Pappy might as well have been in possession of his own time machine because when those players arrived on the playing field, they found themselves in another time and dimension, but little did they know their newly acquired game was as old as the hills.

After the game on the racetrack was finished, the players would stack their peggy sticks in one corner of the garage, congregate on the porch, and discuss their adventures before they left to go home. This is where I saw their excited, happy, beaming young faces giving their personal post-game reviews. This was truly a work of art, magnificently orchestrated by the master peggy player.

I fully understood because at one time I happened to be one of those young faces. I wondered how many different generations of boys Pappy had transformed in this fashion, and regardless of age, those boys would never forget the first time they played peggy.

While I was growing up, I had asthma, and I remember Mom draping a towel over my head while I would breathe in the fumes coming out of a vaporizer. Dogwood was used for many things, for slingshots, peggys, and peggy sticks, but there was one application where a dogwood stick was used as a cure for asthma.

I do not know the origin of this belief; maybe it was an old Indian remedy or something that was passed down over the years. My parents measured me against the wall, and Pappy went down to the woods and cut a dogwood stick a few inches taller than I was.

The belief was when I grew to the length of the stick, my asthma would vanish and be absorbed by the stick. This stick was hung over my bedroom door, and when the affliction went away, the stick would be thrown out. Several other ballplayers shared Pappy's belief and did the same for their children. I think I just outgrew the ailment, but this ritual was rather bizarre, and its origin still remains a mystery.

Chapter 28

Baseball Mentorship

Shad and Vernon worked with and trained many ballplayers up through the years. Their more significant ball-playing proteges were Robert Stallings, Richard Lefler, and myself.

Fletch and Roxy Stallings owned and ran a convenience store, called Stallings Grocery, at the corner of Highland Avenue and Poplar Street. Their son, Robert Stallings, was a left-handed pitcher who happened to be playing for Hartsell High School at the time under Coach Cliff Evans, another player who had played with Pappy with the Concord Patriots in '52. Cliff told Robert if he wanted to learn about baseball, he should go see Shad Whittington.

Not too many coaches would send their ballplayers for someone else to train. Almost every weekend, Robert would come up to see Pappy, and they would work together in the front yard. Their practice sessions happened day after day until Pappy thought Robert was ready. Robert Stallings said, "Shad taught me everything I knew about baseball."

Vernon Ford, who happened to be umpiring baseball games at the time, mentored Richard Lefler on the Franklin Mill Hill.

Vernon would give his leftover game balls to Richard so he could practice.

Richard told me a story about the time when he was pitching to his brother in the front yard. Richard was very tall and had a mean fast ball. He wound up and let go of one of his fast balls, and the pitch came in so fast his brother failed to catch the pitch, and the ball hit their family dog in the head and killed it. Richard said, "I was so mad at my brother because I really liked that dog."

Richard was a senior at Hartsell when I started my first year playing Little League baseball with the Hartsell Bulldogs. Richard was the first high school baseball player to hit a home run off the Hartsell Gym. That same year Richard pitched a perfect game against Parkwood High School during a home game. So with the combination of Robert Stallings and Richard Lefler on the mound, it was understandable that the Hartsell High School team had a winning season.

After Richard graduated from Hartsell, he signed with a Baltimore Orioles farm team. When he came back home for visits, he would play on Red McClamrock's team. Red was a left-handed fireball pitcher. When Richard and Red teamed together, they were called Koufax and Drysdale because of the success Sandy Koufax and Don Drysdale had with the Los Angeles Dodgers. Richard Lefler was the last of the great pitchers that came off the Franklin Mill Hill.

Many fans and spectators would talk about the natural talent of ballplayers. Some imagined that a player just woke up one day and do amazing things. However, they did not see the hours and years of practice or the discipline required behind the scenes to hone those skills.

Pappy had given up playing baseball by the time I came along, so sadly enough, I never got to see him play. Between the time Pap quit playing and the time I started, the national pastime was in decline, especially in our area, and many have speculated various reasons for this decline.

One belief was that television was a major nemesis because fans preferred to stay at home and watch Major League games rather than go out to see the local teams play. Others felt that the increasing popularity of slow-pitch softball, especially among the younger players, was ruining the desire and the arms of the future baseball players. Slow-pitch softball, originally designed for aging baseball players, began to increase in popularity and was spreading like wildfire in our region. Many players left baseball to play slow-pitch softball.

Other competition was high school and college football; they drew larger crowds and took in more revenue. Stock car and drag-racing was also very prevalent, and its popularity was on a meteoric rise.

Although those reasons all have their merit, I believe the major reason for the decline was one of economics. The mills and other industrial businesses stopped sponsoring baseball teams in and around 1959. This marked a major change because baseball and the textile mills had been synonymous since the turn of the century.

It was unfair for the mill workers to have to compete with the semipro ballplayers to receive equal pay, so the mills stopped sponsoring ballplayers and teams. Without the sponsorship and financial support of the textile or industrial leagues, the men's adult baseball league took a nosedive.

The baseball players from this time forward would arise from the school systems. There were a few locally sponsored teams that remained, and those sponsors could claim travel, supplies, and advertising tax write-offs but not at the scale that the textile industry could provide. This marked the beginning of the end of men's adult semipro baseball.

Pap and Red McClamrock admired and respected each other. They had a lot in common: Both were competitors, both had hot tempers, and they were good at what they did. You would think like charges would repel, but this was not the case because catchers liked good pitchers and vice versa. Pappy had great respect for those who were good at their craft, and Red was a pitcher of Major League material.

Red had a quick temper, and from some of the stories I have heard, he could whip half of a ball team and if he had time to catch his breath, would whip the other half. However, Red was well respected in the community, and if he had to fight, it was understood that his opponent probably deserved it. I was also told, "Whatever you do, don't get in the car with Red because he drives like a madman."

Red worked for Douglas Aircraft at the Charlotte Airport and lived on Branch Drive. Red and his wife Helen had four children: three boys and a girl. Kenny came first, and then Reggie followed six minutes later. Rick came a year later; Rick and I were about the same age, and we shared some classes together in high school, so I knew him better than the others. Their sister, Lisa, was the youngest.

Brother Ted moved next door to the McClamrocks in 1965, and although I had met those boys on the ball field, I became much closer after Ted and Red became neighbors. Whenever I visited Ted, in no time at all, I would end up next door with the McClamrock boys. We pitched horseshoes, played basketball, but our main stay was baseball. Kenny was my shortstop for three seasons in high school. Reggie was my catcher in Babe Ruth at Hartsell up through my junior year in high school.

One Saturday evening in November, Ted happened to be washing and waxing his black 1956 Chevrolet when Red stepped out in the backyard and asked Ted, "Do you want to go for a drive with me over to Kannapolis?"

Ted answered, "No, Red, I have to finish waxing my car, maybe some other time."

Nobody knows the details, but at four o'clock the following morning, Red ended up in a violent car wreck. The highway patrolman who responded estimated that Red was traveling over a hundred miles per hour when he clipped a telephone pole, hit a cedar tree, rolled through a fence, and slammed into a large oak tree.

A man came out in his front yard and saw Red McClamrock inside the wrecked car. Red raised his hand and tried to speak, then his arm fell, and he never got the words out of his mouth. Red was not wearing a seat belt, so he was thrown around inside the car so violently, his body could not take the abuse. The next day Pappy drove me over to the accident site. I really didn't want to go because I admired Mr. McClamrock.

The wake and the funeral ceremony were held, and there were throngs of ballplayers and family members present. The ballplayers finally learned that Red's real name was Harold Kenneth McClamrock. Our community was very much intertwined with baseball.

Mrs. McClamrock, Helen, Red's wife, worked at the Cabarrus County Courthouse for years and raised those four children by herself. Her son, Rick, asked his mom in later years why she never remarried. Mrs. McClamrock answered with, "Son, when I saw your daddy for the first time, in his uniform on that ball field, I knew he was the only man for me."

I played my first official Little League baseball game at Randolph Field during the summer of 1964. I was ten years old at the time. We were the Hartsell Bulldogs, and my first coach was Harold Mauney, Willard, and Richard's younger brother.

They put me in the outfield, and I was pretty shaky, so they moved me behind the plate then over to first base. I wore number 4 on the back of my jersey, same as Lou Gehrig. However, being the son of a prominent ballplayer, my training started many years before I ever donned a uniform.

There were many sessions out in the backyard where Pappy would catch with me. Notice I didn't say play catch because it started out as play, but it immediately progressed into a something more serious. During those sessions, he taught me to throw with my wrist and body by getting my body into position before I threw the ball.

He taught me how to backhand stab a ground ball. While the other parents and coaches were teaching their kids and players to catch a ball with two hands, Pappy taught me to catch balls with only the glove hand, with the arm fully extended, and then crow hop and accelerate my body behind the throw with a wrist snap at the end.

He taught me to run on my toes and not flat-footed, so the fly balls or line drives that I was trying to catch would not appear to hop up and down. It was a smooth approach to the ball. He also told me to breathe in through my nose and out through my mouth while I was running.

Hitting was even more advanced. He would have me stand beside the cinder block garage with a sawed-off mop handle, and he would throw a red rubber ball from half the pitching distance. The Little League pitching rubber was forty-six feet, so he was only twenty-two feet away, and I had less than a second to locate and hit the ball. The ball would be by me before I could even get my stick around. He would say, "Look at my hand." Then he added, "Now don't hit the ball back at me," and after I missed about twenty pitches in a row, I told him, "Don't worry Pap, I won't."

One day he started talking about the slot. The slot is an imaginary point between the hitter and the pitcher, where the batter's strike zone is projected out from the plate. The farther out the point is, depending on the speed of the pitch, the smaller this zone becomes. Sometimes the point is the size of a basketball and only halfway or three quarters of the way to the pitcher. If the pitcher was fast, the point might go all the way to the pitcher's hand, at his release point.

If the pitch was in the slot, you knew in advance the pitch was going to be a strike, so the hitter should start his swing. As the ball gets closer, the hitter should pick up the spin on the ball and adjust his swing accordingly. If the pitch had back spin, like a fast ball, the hitter was supposed to hit the top part of the ball, but if it had a forward spin, like a curve, the hitter was supposed to hit the bottom of the ball. He preached that all good hitters need to have excellent bat speed.

The hitter should be totally relaxed while the pitch is coming in, "loose as a goose," but when the ball is about to be hit was when the hitter should tighten up, including the forearms, through the hips, and all the way down to the leg that pushes off. Then immediately after you hit the ball, the hitter should relax and concentrate on running the bases. It took eleven more seasons of ball playing to understand what he was telling me.

We played most of our Little League games at Gibson Field, not knowing at the time the historical significance of this field. We didn't realize that we were playing on a ball field that had been in existence for sixty-four years.

The Gibson Mill was one of the first mills in Concord to build a housing project around the mill. They also carved out a space so the mill workers could enjoy a recreation area. Gibson Field was not big enough for the men's baseball park, but it was large enough so the men could play their fast-pitch softball games.

The field that I was playing on in 1964 was the same field where Pappy used to pitch fast-pitch in the late '30s. It just so happens that the dimensions of the men's fast-pitch field were the same dimensions as that of a Little League Baseball Field, including sixty feet in between the bases and forty-six feet between home plate and the pitcher's rubber. So one could see that when the men's fast-pitch leagues died out, this field was converted to a Little League Baseball Field without the loss of any real estate.

Jim Helms became our Little League coach during the '65 and '66 seasons. He worked with the boys club in Concord. Coach Helms realized that I was not going to be another catcher like Shad because I was bat blind. It is a natural tendency for anyone to blink or shut their eyes when something comes close to their face or when you think something is going to hit you in one or both of your eyes. Every time the batter would swing at the pitch, I would shut my eyes and lose track of the pitch that was coming in' Experienced catchers can discipline themselves not to fall prey to this natural tendency, but I never did, so they moved me from behind the plate, and I started playing the outfield, pitching and playing first base.

As far back as 1947, baseball integrated when Branch Rickey signed Jackie Robinson with the Brooklyn Dodgers. The United States Army integrated during the Korean War and twenty years after Jackie signed with the Dodgers. The North Carolina school system finally made the change when I was in the seventh grade at Hartsell. Now talented black players could be added to our rosters.

Pappy was not a prejudiced man; he recruited and tried to get black talent added to his baseball teams from all over the state, just like Branch Rickey had done. Pappy was in favor of integration many years before the country was willing to accept the idea. This might explain why the Brooklyn Dodgers was his favorite team and why he chose to swing a thirty-six-inch Larry Doby baseball bat.

It was common knowledge that Pappy, Howard Hooks, or Red McClamrock could play for black teams whenever they chose, but unfortunately, when the black players tried to play on white teams, they would be met with a wall of opposition.

Bryant Parnell told me, "My grandfather Fred Parnell (who played with Pappy in the old Norcott Mill days) would sometimes be denied access to some ball fields because of his dark complexion."

When the managers and team owners shot Pappy's ideas for new talent down, he became angry and answered them with, "I don't play baseball to fill the stands, I play baseball to win, and they'll come a day when you wished that you had too."

I can proudly say that time happened during my generation.

By the time I reached the seventh grade, I had built a decent baseball reputation of my own and was mentioned quite regularly in the sports section of the *Concord Tribune.* After all, Mr. Lapish was my Babe Ruth baseball coach, and Mr. Cliff Evans was our school principal, two baseball players who had played with Pappy with the Concord Patriots in '52.

However, anytime any of Pappy's group would read or talk about my baseball exploits, they would say, "Hey, Shad's boy did it again," or "Did you see what Shad's boy did the other day at Hartsell?"

It was never Harold Whittington that did those things, just Shad's boy.

My petty jealously was laid to rest one day in 196. Just before I stepped out on the front porch, I saw a guy sitting on the steps, listening to one of Pappy's stories. I lingered behind the screen door for quite a while, and I could tell, by the look on the man's face, that he was mesmerized by what Shad was telling him.

A little bit later, a car pulled up in the driveway, and Pappy caught the interest of the next fellow, then another car pulled in, then yet another, and pretty soon our driveway looked like a parking lot, and the porch was full of people.

Pappy talked about a wide array of subjects, from baseball to cotton mills, to hunting and fishing, to WW2, and so forth. When Pap told a story, he could imitate almost any sound or any person he was describing, and he could weave in and out of one story to the next as easy as a mockingbird could switch stanzas during an imitation spree. Pappy was a master storyteller, a raconteur without equal.

At one moment, he would have those guys on the porch almost to the point of tears, and just a few moments later, he would have them laughing so hard, they would be rolling on the ground in fits of laughter.

I stayed behind the screen door and marveled at this spectacle and realized that those visitors and many others in our area considered my father to be a legend. So I didn't mind being called Shad's boy after that experience.

Pappy loved to watch TV, and he watched the Three Stooges, Laurel and Hardy, and the Funny Man on a regular basis. But when the baseball game came on, that was a different story. Most other viewers would just sit and enjoy the game, whereas Pappy would critique every play and would talk to the television like it was another person.

One summer day in 1969, on the way to Hipp-MacBride's Sporting Goods store, I asked Pappy what he thought about the astronauts who landed on the moon. He said, "Hell, I don't know why anybody would want to go to the moon. You can't grow anything up there, and you can't even breathe up there."

Sometimes Pappy was just as entertaining as Lowell Ferguson's talking bird about certain things.

During my sophomore year at Central, on February 6, 1970, Richard Mauney, Pappy's lifelong friend died. He lived in Albemarle, and they said he collapsed in the bathroom while shaving. This hit home for Pap, and he took the news really hard.

When the 1970 high school baseball season began, our team started to gel, mainly because of the excellent coaching and mentoring that was delivered by Coach Jerry Pierce. I was privileged to have pitched nine games that season, with seven wins and two losses.

There were several reasons I attribute to those victories, which include the countless sessions Mr. Pierce had me pitch to him while he was behind the plate. Mr. Pierce was a top-notch catcher and knew how to make his pitchers work. Our team had good defensive players, and we had good hitters.

In those days, a pitcher was not limited by a pitch count, and it was expected for a starting pitcher to end the seven inning game unless something went terribly wrong. I had Richard Lefler to thank for my three-quarter-armed sinking fast ball and Mr. Lapish's overhand curve called a drop. The most effective pitch that I used was the two-fingered knuckleball that Howard Hooks taught me how to throw.

But Pappy taught me that when you pitched, you had to think like a hitter and not deliver the pitch he wanted to see. Isn't it uncanny how the culmination of bits and pieces from other people's lives can make such a difference?

As the 1970 season melted away, and my sophomore year was finished, I went bream fishing with Vernon Ford and Pappy at this two-acre farm pond somewhere near Mount Pleasant. Roger Strube, Johnson's nephew, a senior at Central, and another baseball player who grew up on the Franklin Mill Hill, drove out to meet us with an urgent message from Coach Jerry Pierce.

Roger walked over to me and said, "There is going to be a sports banquet at Central Cabarrus, and Mr. Pierce wants you to be there tonight."

Pappy and Vernon started reeling in their lines, and this was the first time I have ever seen them cut any of their fishing trips short. They drove me back home. I cleaned up and changed, then Pappy drove me out to Central, and to my surprise, Coach Jerry Pierce presented me with the team's Most Valuable Player trophy.

I was nervous when they snapped the picture of me holding the trophy, but I was thinking of Richard Mauney, Pappy's lifelong friend, the entire time. Somehow I felt that I had won the trophy for him that night, and I wished that he could have been there. Richard was the only Hartsell School baseball pitcher who made it to the Major Leagues.

In April 1971, Charles A. Cannon, the textile mill baron, died of a massive stroke. It was a major event for those of Pappy's era. There were those who viewed Cannon as a rich miser who made millions from the sweat of his workers' brows; however, there were many others who were thankful of the opportunities of employment. Had they looked upon the man's life and his family's contributions for the people of North and South Carolina, they might have come away with a better-rounded picture.

The Cannons provided jobs and affordable living quarters for thousands of workers in North Carolina, South Carolina, and Georgia. They built a textile industry that was world-renowned; his family built the city of Kannapolis in 1906, the largest unincorporated city in the world. He backed North and South Carolina banks that would have otherwise folded during the Great Depression, so most of the New Deal policies that prevailed throughout other areas of the nation were not needed.

I have heard of stories where Charlie Cannon made deals with members of the black market just so his workers would have shoes for the winter. Without the Cannons and others like them, the Carolina Textile Baseball League would not have existed, and the professional Independent Carolina Baseball League would not have been possible. The Cabarrus Memorial Hospital, where I was born in 1954, drew their checks from Cannon Mills, so the influence of Cannon Mills was a mainstay in our area, a historical achievement that will probably never be equaled again in the Southeast. When Charles Albert Cannon died, an entire way of making a living started to die as well.

While I was a junior at Central Cabarrus, the season of 1971 marked another winning year. This was my first season of American Legion Baseball with Post 51 in Concord. We played our home games at Webb Field, the same ball field where the Concord Weavers played with the Independent Carolina League from 1936 to 1938, the same field where Richard Mauney used to pitch in Victory League in '43, and where Pappy, Vernon Ford, and Johnnie Clark used to play with the Concord Patriots in '52.

By the time I started playing, the bank in left and center field had been replaced by concrete bleachers, so the plays that Willard Mauney used to make on the left field bank was no longer possible.

When I pitched at Webb Field, sometimes my mind would briefly slip off into the past, where I could imagine all the images of those who played before me. Yet I could still focus on the game being played in the present. In between pitches, I happened to notice a new group of ball chasers standing on the outside of the chain-link fence that ran parallel to Two Mile Branch out by right field. Those ball chasers would replace my generation of ballplayers in the future.

During some home games at Central Cabarrus, Pappy and Willard Mauney would show up to see me play. Willard told me before one game, "One day, when you are pitching in the Majors, you will look over in the stands and see two gray-haired old men, and that will be me and your daddy."

That was quite a compliment coming from a professional ballplayer of many years. Willard and Pappy did not give out too many compliments.

The most cherished baseball memory from my high school baseball days happened at a home game at Central. Pappy and Vernon Ford were sitting on the top row of bleachers, just behind our bench. During my first trip to the plate, I hit a line drive over the pitcher's left shoulder, and the ball crossed over the center field fence and left the park at the same altitude. It was a shot, and it happened to be my first high school home run. This home run stood out among the other home runs that followed because Pappy and Vernon, two of the foremost home run kings from the area, got to see me do it. I will carry that special memory with me to my grave.

Chapter 29

Carolina Seen from Afar

When the newscasters were covering the Vietnam conflict on TV was when Pappy would really get fired up. You could see his expressions change, and his face would turn red. He would start cussing and yelling at the TV. I have heard him say many times, "Vietnam, that ain't no damn war. We could take the home guard (National Guard) over there and whoop that bunch in six months."

I didn't want him to get all worked up, so I would say, "It's okay, Pap, everything is going to be all right."

Later in life, I realized that he was right because he had fought in a World War without restrictions, a time when there was no substitute for total victory.

Vietnam was another example of the world powers not fighting directly against one another, but through the influence and at the expense of third-world countries. I think he was really worried about my possible involvement if the conflict dragged out any longer.

By the time I hit that home run at Central, I had already signed up as a part of the Delayed Enlistment Program for the United States Air Force. I had participated in the Central Cabarrus Air

Force Junior ROTC program. Since Mr. Pierce left during my sophomore year, I lacked the proper guidance required to peruse a baseball scholarship. The decision to join the military was greatly influenced by the naval stories and adventures that Pappy, my brothers JM and Ted had told me when I was growing up.

I was not yet ready to leave the day I was supposed to go to Charlotte and sign in at the induction center. I lingered awhile in the bathroom that morning, opened up the medicine cabinet, and just started reminiscing because almost every item in that cabinet had a memory associated with it.

On the upper left-hand corner of the top shelf was a glass of water that held Pappy's upper set of false teeth, which he soaked at night. Pappy didn't have a lower set of teeth, which explained why he preferred to eat only soft foods. Next to the glass was a shaving brush, and beside the shaving brush was a tube of shaving cream.

Men from Pappy's generation used a brush and a shaving cup that contained shaving soap, and after adding warm water, they would stir with the brush until they had a soapy lather to apply on their face. However, Pappy would just squirt a little cream onto his brush and then run water on the brush and lather up.

His shaving utensil was an old Gillette double-edged razor, which opened at the top. The same style razor was standard issue found in the army packs in WW1. The first time I used his razor, I cut myself in so many places, and after I placed little patches of toilet paper on the cuts, I looked like someone suffering from a severe case of smallpox.

The septic stick was the first item on the second shelf, and this was the torture device that you were supposed to use if you cut yourself while shaving. If you have ever used a septic stick, you would vow never to cut yourself shaving ever again because it burned like hell. If you really felt brave, you could splash on your face alcohol from the bottle that was beside the septic stick.

First aid was simple-we had a small tin of Band-Aids, a round roll of white tape, a bottle of mercurochrome, and a brown bottle of hydrogen peroxide. The roll of white tape was used more on baseball bats and peggy sticks than for cuts and scrapes.

The next item on the shelf was a bottle of Vaseline Hair Tonic. I used to slick my hair down with this tonic before I combed my hair, using a long barber's rat-tailed comb. There were times after I came out of the bathroom, Pappy would say that I looked like Alfalfa from the Little Rascals or Adolph Hitler, which used to irritate the hell out of me.

Pappy was bald on top but grew his hair long enough on the sides so he could comb his hair over to cover the bald spot. You might see him sitting in the porch swing without wearing some type of cap or hat, but before he left the house, he usually wore a baseball cap or a dress hat similar to the type that Coach Bear Bryant was usually seen wearing.

There was a long silver tube of something located on the bottom shelf of the medicine cabinet. It had been there so long; the label had worn off. Brother Ted was the only one besides Pappy who knew the actual contents of this tube. After Ted returned from taking a cross-country motorcycle ride, from California to North Carolina, he was heavily chapped and raw around his crotch area because he was wearing his leathers. Carolinians would have said, "He was gaulded."

After Ted got out of the shower and dried off, he grabbed the silver tube and squeezed some of the cream into his hand and rubbed it on the raw spot on the right side. Then he repeated the exercise on the left side of his crotch, and the ingredients started to take effect. The burning started, and Ted ran from one wall to the next, screaming, because he realized that the mystery tube happened to be Deep Heat mentholatum rub. After that reflection, I closed the medicine cabinet door and felt that I was ready to leave home and join the United States Air Force.

The bus that took me from Concord to the Charlotte Induction Center was a short ride compared to the bus ride I was scheduled to take later to Lackland AFB, near San Antonio, Texas, the longest distance I had ever traveled away from home up to at that point. Oh, I had visited Tennessee, Virginia, and South Carolina, but nothing compared to the journeys I was about to take during my tour with the air force.

Servicemen and women who were my contemporaries still traveled by bus or drove their own vehicles to their stateside assignments and were flown to their overseas assignments.

Servicemen from Pappy's generation traveled mostly by train and boarded ships to make their destinations overseas.

Basic training was the main trust of my life for six weeks, and after finishing high school and playing for the Concord Post 51 American Legion team would be the only ball playing that I did during the 1972 season.

The basic trainees would get to call home every now and then, and we stood in line and to wait our turn to use the pay phone. After you join the military, you learn how to stand in line. I would use my loose change I had saved to pay for the call because I didn't want to burden my parents with collect calls. Our home phone had only been installed two years earlier, when I was a junior in high school.

To save on phone bills, some residents chose party lines, which were cheaper than the private lines, but the party lines would have to be shared with several other households along the street. This posed a problem because some users were phone hogs and would tie up the phone for hours, especially if Mrs. Smith and Mrs. Jones got to talking. Mrs. Smith and Mrs. Jones lived across the street from each other and could have had their conversations on the front porch, but they chose to use the phone instead.

While using these party lines, there were times when you would be on the phone, and you could hear someone else pick up their receiver to listen in on your conversation. Pappy didn't want any part of those party lines, so he chose to get the more expensive private line installed. He said, "I don't want any of them damn lip-flapping busybodies to know what the hell I'm talkin' about."

After basic training, I was assigned to a technical school at Chanute Air Force Base, near Rantoul, Illinois, scheduled from the end of the summer to graduate in early December 1972. Although I was farther away from Lake Michigan than Pappy was when he was in the navy, I could feel the bitter cold, similar to what he had felt when he was training near the Great Lakes during WW2.

With my tech school completed, I took a short leave, went back home, and then drove my car to my first permanent assignment to Upper State New York at Plattsburgh AFB. My specialty was to work on the FB-111, and I was proud to be assigned to an elite strategic air command base.

Upper State New York was even colder than the area around the Great Lakes, especially when the west winds blew across Lake Champlain. I can recall one night we experienced temperatures that dipped as low as sixty degrees below zero with the chill factor.

We were well dressed and equipped for the cold, and we received training in case we experienced a blizzard at the base. When spring rolled around and the snow melted was when I was introduced to a fantastic game called fast-pitch softball.

Fast-pitch softball was no longer played during my time in Carolina. Men's fast-pitch had actually died out sometime after 1947 in the area and was rarely played by most civilian teams east of the Mississippi River. However, the military played fast-pitch softball all across the country and overseas. The game was much more intense than slow-pitch, even though slow-pitch softball was sweeping the nation like a storm.

So as a nineteen-year-old, I made our squadron team and got to experience the same type ball playing that Pappy had played during the late 1930s and early 1940s. During my first season, I was fortunate enough to play for the Plattsburg Air Force Base Team.

The base team was like the Major Leagues. We got to play teams in our local area and other base teams, such as Pease AFB in New Hampshire. They would put us on the manifest of a C-130, a C-141, or a KC-135 and fly us to the base. Those aircraft were scheduled to fly to those other bases, run parts or perform aerial refueling en route, so we were just additional passengers who happened to be on the manifest. Why, even the Major Leaguers didn't get to see F-111s, B-52s, or F4s, being refueled en route to their baseball games. That was quite an experience for a Carolina boy from the sticks.

Our base team played against a very formidable local powerhouse civilian team, called Ausable Acres, north of Keeseville, New York. Many of the players spoke more French than they did English, and several of those ballplayers were retired Major League baseball players. Two of them had played for the New York Yankees.

When we played on base at Plattsburgh, the level of play was only at the intermural level, and the pitchers only had control of two pitches, usually a drop and a change-up; however, the base level pitchers were much better, and the pitchers threw a mean rise ball.

Coming out of baseball, it was common to hit a pitch that was going down because of the height of the mound in baseball, but in fast-pitch, the pitcher was level with the hitter, and his release point was beside the hip. There is no way a baseball pitcher could throw a pitch that could start low in the strike zone, and by the time the pitch got to the hitter, it would be shoulder to neck high. I could hit the intermediate pitchers well, but against the dominant rise ball, I set a strike-out record that season.

Furthermore, those pitchers at the base level, especially Ausable Acres, would leap off the rubber and cut the distance from forty-six feet down to forty feet, giving less time for the hitter to react. In fast pitch-softball, there is no such thing as a fast ball. All the pitches, except for a change-up, came at top speed, and each pitch would move from its normal plane. If a pitcher threw a ball that didn't move, it would be a serious mistake.

It was irritating and quite embarrassing when it came time to shake the player's hands from the Ausable Acres team after they beat us. The only thing the pitchers could say in English was "good game" with their French Canadian accents. Even though I became the strike-out king that season, I still wished that Pappy would have been there to see me play.

The highlight of the '73 softball season was when the Queen and her maids came to Ausable Acres to play against an army of all stars, comprised of a combination of local and Plattsburgh base team players.

The Queen, Rosie Black, was surrounded by only three other players, all female, or at least we thought were female. Those four players had to cover the entire field, similar to what the King and his court would do. The Queen was an outstanding pitcher and could throw about seventeen different pitches, but the pitch that messed the hitters up the most was the one she threw between her legs.

After the game started, I could not help but notice the woman who played first base named Lotta Chatter. Something wasn't right with her; in fact, the first baseman was actually the pitcher's brother

Norm Beaird dressed in drag. It was more of a show than a softball game, and the Ausable Acers All Stars ended up winning, but if the Queen would have had a full complement of players, I am sure the outcome of the game would have been quite different.

I lived in the barracks the first year at Plattsburgh and would use the phone at the end of the hall to call home on the weekends. During one of those calls, sometime in 1973, my parents told me that Vernon Ford had died of bone cancer. The tragic news hurt me deeply.

I could not sleep at all that night because I reviewed all my memories of Uncle Bubby, from the time he picked me up and placed me on his shoulders when I was a toddler through the years we spent together fishing on the Santee River and at Carolina Beach, all the way to his visits to the baseball field at Central to see me play. However, I knew something was wrong with Uncle Bubby long before I left high school.

I believe there were physical secrets that were never discussed, or maybe Vernon Ford was in denial. First, he was denied entry into the military during WW2 because he failed the entrance physical. Nobody knew why because it was never discussed.

His cousin Bill Ford told me that "Vernon would hurt himself just by sliding into a base and would be black and blue for days afterward."

Howard Hooks Sr. and Vernon wanted to see who could punch the hardest by hitting each other in the shoulder. Howard punched Vernon, and then Vernon said, "I have to stop because you broke my arm."

There was also the contest where Vernon fought the chimpanzee in 1959 beside the fairgrounds, where he was hospitalized with a broken collar bone. Even though Vernon Ford appeared as bigger than life, he was a very fragile man.

I can remember another time when I was in the fourth or fifth grade; Pappy told me Uncle Bubby was in the hospital because he was involved in a car wreck. So he drove us over to visit Vernon, but Pappy would not let me go up in his room. I stayed by the car on the back side of the hospital. Then I saw a window open on the third floor, and I could see Uncle Bubby waving at me. I yelled up to him and asked, "Where did you get hurt, Uncle Bubby?"

He bent his arm and stuck his elbow out the window, and I could see a big bandage was placed between his right elbow and wrist. I still believe that this incident was not because of a car wreck.

Richard Lefler told me many years later he attended to Vernon during those heartbreaking last days. Richard said, "It was hard for me to see such a big and powerful man slowly dwindle to an eighty-pound skeleton."

I was glad I didn't have to see those things Richard had experienced, that a man I admired and loved would have to die that way. I am sure that there were many my age and younger consumed by tears of love and grief when their "Uncle Bubby" passed away. He will forever be a champion to the children who knew him.

The same day I found out Vernon had died, a fellow serviceman was practicing on his piano. All of us could hear his somber music resonate down the halls and the stairways of the barracks. I just sat in my room and listened. The piece of music was especially fitting for the mood I was in. I haven't heard another classical piece of music that so accurately described the emotions I was feeling since that time. It reached down deep and spoke directly to my soul.

It wasn't until many years later when I learned the title of the piece of music the serviceman was practicing. It happened to be the first movement of Ludwig van Beethoven's "Moonlight Sonata." It was as if Beethoven himself was saying goodbye to Vernon. Even today, whenever I hear that beautiful classical piece, my thoughts and emotions return to that sad day in the Plattsburgh barracks.

Plattsburgh was followed by an overseas assignment to Korat, Thailand, where we played quite a bit of fast-pitch softball; then a return stateside to Nellis AFB, near Las Vegas, Nevada, where I organized a handpicked team of all stars, that took on all challengers in baseball, fast and slow-pitch softball. Finally, I left the USAF and returned home to North Carolina, to the life I had left behind.

After I arrived back in Carolina, I was offered an opportunity to try out, as a walk on for the Charlotte Hornets baseball team, but the salary offered was not enough to support a family of three. I happened to be faced with the same situation my father and many of the Franklin Mill ballplayers had to face during their era. So I never took advantage of the tryout.

One day, out of the blue, Pappy wanted me to go over to Hipp-MacBride's Sporting Goods store to pick up three new baseballs and a thirty-six-inch bat. Then he said, "I know you are becoming a good pitcher, and I want to see if I can get any hits off you."

He asked Ted to come along, and Ted suited up as the catcher. This contest took place down at Hartsell Field.

This was quite a shock because I had never seen Pappy hit a baseball as far back as I could remember. After I warmed up, he took a couple of practice swings, stepped up to the plate, and told me, "Now don't hold back."

This kindled the old Whittington ire within me, so I wound up and released a ninety-plus-mile-per-hour fast ball.

Pappy connected with this pitch, about chest high, and he pulled it foul down the right field line. He hit it over the oak trees on the hill, along the right field line, and it ended up on the other side of Swink Street. After the ball hit on the other side of the street, Pappy said, "Damn, I was a little out in front of that one."

In other words, my fast ball was too slow for him.

The amazing part of this feat was when this contest took place, he was sixty-two, and I was twenty-two. I continued to pitch to him, and he belted head-high line drives to all parts of Hartsell Field that day. I was humbled once again. As we were walking up the bank in left field, he looked at me and said, "Once could always could."

Chapter 30

A Tragic Event

My stay in North Carolina lasted only eleven months. During that time, I was employed as a concrete worker for Raymond Hatley, and I ran slubbers at the Norcott Mill, just like Pappy used to do.

During that baseball season, I played with a very good baseball team called Midland Tigers. I happened to be the only white player on the team. Of all the years I have spent on ball fields, I never enjoyed playing with any other team as much as I did when I played for Coach Benny Love and the Midland Tigers.

We were much better than the other teams, and it reminded me of the movie *Bingo Long's Traveling All Stars.* The shenanigans that took place on and off the field were much more comical than anything the movie had to offer, and I was surrounded by excellent athletes.

However, through all this enjoyment, I felt that something was missing, for I had had a taste of the world and wanted to find employment that offered better pay and adventure, so I decided to rejoin the military. When I reentered, I signed up to be a US Army as an infantry paratrooper. It has been said that it takes a crazy person to jump out of a perfectly good aircraft, but that did not lessen my resolve.

Pappy tried to talk me out of joining such a rough group; he said, "They are a bunch of killers," and they were quite notorious during WW2 and many years thereafter.

He knew that his goal of turning me into a Major League baseball player was starting to slip away.

He added that I could play college baseball, but he didn't realize that I had not taken the required preparatory courses to attend college. Mom was sad because I was leaving, but she believed that if I was going to make something out of my life, I had to get away from Concord to do so.

While I was away, things with the family remained the same. Brother Ted still resided on Branch Drive, Pappy worked as a slubber hand in Kannapolis, and Mom was still with the sheet department at Plant 1 in Kannoplis.

Eva had just graduated from high school. She was a basketball player and a cheerleader and had just started dating. Before I left to enlist in the army, I recall that she had invited her boyfriend over one evening. She had prepared a meal and was setting the table when Mom told me that Eva had her date coming over, that I was to be nice and not to bother them. That was good advice, but I didn't always follow good advice.

Before her date arrived, Eva had set an elaborate table, she had a very nice dress on, and she was wearing her hair like Julia Roberts. The only problem was that she wanted me to join them at the dinner table, so she fixed a plate for me as well.

I was supposed to eat with them, chat for a while, then I was to move out to the front porch swing so they could be alone. I forget exactly what she had prepared, I think it was chicken, and I saw her pouring big glasses of chocolate milk. She was going all out to impress her date. I knew that I could make Eva bust out laughing at any time, and the chocolate milk gave me an idea.

I chose the right moment to make my play. Just as Eva was taking a big gulp of chocolate milk, I made a gesture that caused Eva to laugh, and she spewed milk all over the table. She became very upset and almost started to cry. Her date thought it was pretty good. After all, isn't that what big brothers are supposed to do?

While stationed at Fort Bragg, North Carolina, I lived in a small apartment in the Bordeaux area in Fayetteville. Heavy snow had fallen that day that blanketed the Piedmont region in North Carolina. While I was driving around town, I noticed a snipe standing in the snow, gently rocking back and forth.

I watched the bird for quite some time and thought this was unusual behavior. We had hunted snipe many times along the Carolina creek beds and cane fields. I took it as a sign, and it was not the first time I received premonitions from animals that something was wrong, nor would it be the last; however, I didn't know what this meant until later on that night.

About the same time that I spotted the snipe, a tragic event was unfolding on Gold Hill Road, just before the road crossed Buffalo Creek. My sister lost control of her Mercury Bobcat in a snow drift along the road. She spun off the road, barely missing the bridge abutment, and ended up splashing into the creek.

I was still unaware of this even after we had gone to bed, when my wife and I heard a knock at the door, which woke us up. My wife answered the door, but no one was there. She returned to bed and told me the news. I was still groggy and not fully awake, and I told her that in my mind's eye, I could see Jesus knocking on our door. This was another strange message. The knock at the door was probably someone from my unit trying to deliver the dire news. A few moments later, we got a call from Mom, stating that Eva had been involved in an accident and was in the hospital.

The unit granted me a short leave, and I headed home. When I arrived at the hospital, I saw Eva stretched out in her room. When I stepped out of the room I was told that her backbone had been severed, and she would never walk again. The other family members were crying, but I was very angry as to what had happened because there had to be an explanation.

The next day I went to the accident site and performed an impromptu accident investigation. Accident investigations help determine what can be corrected in future events; unfortunately, it was too late to prevent the one that had just happened.

The snow had melted by this time, and I could only imagine how many times she spun around before the car left the road. The vehicle left the road, traveled down a twenty-foot bank, crossed a ditch, and I could see where the left front bumper made an impression in the ground on the other side of the ditch.

Then the car catapulted in the air, flipping end over end. As it started flipping, it hooked a barbed wire fence and pulled three fence posts out of the ground. Even though the Bobcat was hung up with this fence, it didn't seem to slow the vehicle down. The vehicle traversed thirty feet across the ground and struck a big oak tree thirty feet in the air then fell into the creek.

After leaving the accident site, I went to examine the damaged car. Pappy and Ted were with me, and while I was checking out the vehicle, I started explaining to Pap and Ted what I thought happened during the accident, and while I was doing so, I could not control my anger and disappointment.

I told Pappy, because Eva was not wearing her seat belt when the car started flipping end over end, she was thrown in the back seat, and when the car hit the oak tree, it crushed the top of the car and also crushed her back. Then I pointed to the top of the vehicle, along the front seat, and told them that this area was not damaged, so the seat belt would have saved her.

I did this because Pappy would not wear seat belts and cut the seat belts out in his car. I also knew that Eva and I drove like race-car drivers, like Pappy.

There were several incidents where I was almost killed driving this way; once, when I spun out of control on a wet curve on the Zion Church Road, with Terry Gledhill and Bill Edwards in the car. There was another time, while driving to school, and I was going so fast, I could not stop in time and ended up in the middle of Highway 49. Had any other vehicle been near those two events, I would probably not be alive today.

I also remember three or four of us riding in the back of Pappy's truck, standing up in the back, while holding on to the top of the truck. Driver's safety has evolved since those days, now they would not even think about doing this today.

All this information might make sense in reality, but I could not determine had she been wearing her seat belt and splashed down in the creek, she might have ended up underwater and would have drowned. This was a fact that I had overlooked. Regardless as to what I thought had happened, divine intervention was the controlling factor.

This was a life-changing event for Eva and the family. Her original plans had to be put on hold, and the mending process was painful and slow. Eva had to stay at home longer, a wheelchair ramp was added to the back porch, and she learned to drive using hand controls. You can read more about her miraculous transformation in Eva's book, *Mae Bell's Daughter.*

After her accident, the church members flocked to her support, and she joined the Fellowship of Christian Athletes. It was amazing to hear that Bobby Richardson, the Yankee second baseman, would stop in and visit her. After he talked to Eva, he would step out on the front porch and exchange baseball stories with Pappy.

Chapter 31

Mae Bell's Final Bout

Many years had passed, and I didn't get the chance to come home as often as I use to. I had a family of my own and was very busy with military activities, which included several overseas assignments, which made trips home impossible.

I remember one time when I did get to visit, Mom and I took a trip to Food Lion to buy groceries. My parents were retired by this time, and they didn't have much money coming in. My goal, like most other men, was to buy the groceries and push the shopping cart. Shopping was and has never been one of my strong points. Mom would go up ahead of me up and down the aisles.

While shopping, I noticed that Mom's hips were not level, and she walked with a lateral sway. I didn't know that she was scheduled for a hip replacement. These symptoms were well known to everyone else, except me, and I was not granted the time to cope with her condition. It was very painful to see her this way.

During our shopping spree, my mind drifted back to something Eva told me during one of our previous phone conversations while I was away. Mom's job was at stake years ago at Cannon Mills. She folded sheets and had done so for God knows how long, but they introduced a folding machine that would do the job that many of the workers had done previously by hand.

They told her she had to learn how to run the machine or be out of a job. Eva could hear Mama crying at night, thinking she would lose her job. Well, Mom mastered the folding machine with flying colors and kept her job with Cannon Mills.

More seriously, several years later, she had the biggest challenge of her life. She had her bout with cancer, which included chemotherapy; during which, she lost her hair. It has been said that a woman's hair is her glory, which was and still is very demoralizing for a woman or for anyone to have to suffer this fate. Once again she persevered through the difficulty.

Six years later, she was scheduled for a doctor's visit and was readmitted to the hospital. Just as time moves on, so did my army career. I had graduated from flight school in 1979 and flew helicopters for the army and had numerous tours; however, during this time, I was now stationed at Fort Campbell, Kentucky. I decided to give Eva a call. Eva told me that Mom was in the hospital and gave me the number to Mom's room. I called Mom, and she told me everything was all right.

After the call was made, a strange thing happened at my house. Outside the bedroom window, a bluebird was desperately trying to get in through the window. I thought this was very strange, and then I thought of a story Pappy had told me about a similar event that took place many years ago on the Franklin Mill Hill. He told about a mill worker who had returned from work and had just put his baby daughter to bed in her crib. He went in his living room, sat down on the couch, and started looking out his picture window. Suddenly, a dove came to the window and started fluttering its wings, just hovering on the other side of the glass.

The man thought this was strange behavior for a bird to want to try to get inside the house. The dove flew away but returned to the window and repeated the same activity as before.

It was at this moment he realized the dove was sending him a message, reminding him to check on his daughter. He returned to the crib and noticed a bubble of blood oozing out of his little girl's nose. She had died of a brain hemorrhage.

It came to me that the bluebird was delivering a message to me. I called my sister and told her to call the hospital and to speak to the head nurse then call me back with the results. This was before the Health Insurance Portability Act (HIPAA) and a patient's medical information was not so heavily guarded.

Not long afterward, Eva did call and told me it was serious, that she was making plans to leave Hopkinsville to see Mom, and I could go after her visit was completed. It didn't take long to notify my unit and arrange for a leave.

The charge nurse had told Eva that although Mom won the original cancer battle, her immune system had been damaged to a point where it was not working the way it should. Her lungs were constantly filling up with fluid, like a bad case of pneumonia. Mom knew her condition was bad but had downplayed her condition when she spoke to us on the phone. Somehow my intuition told me something was happening, but it was the bluebird's message that confirmed my feelings and thoughts.

Eva completed her trip, and it was my turn to visit my old homestead, so I loaded and cranked up the red Jeep Cherokee and was homeward bound. Eventually, I ended up on Interstate 40, a familiar route I had taken so many times before while stationed at Fort Ord, California.

Many military members consider themselves marathon travelers and would boast among our peers how long we could drive. My aviator counterparts traveled mostly at night because of our reverse cycle schedule for flying night unaided and night-vision-goggle flights. We felt more comfortable traveling at night, and there was less traffic to deal with.

However, on this particular trip, the Carolina side of the Appalachians was heavily laden with fog. This proved to be a heavy burden, but I fell in behind an eighteen-wheeler, which had excellent visibility from his high cabin. I followed him through the winding mountain road as if I were flying trail in a formation of helicopters.

This, in the aviation profession, was known as pushing the envelope. I can recall the words of an outstanding mentor and teacher Greg Reese, our instructor pilot and instrument flight examiner, who stated, "A persons' limitations aren't known until that individual's limits have been exceeded."

Pushing the limit was common practice in those days, we felt it was needed at the time. This mindset is not so prevalent today and is seldom practiced, and the need to push the limit no longer seems to exist.

Shooting the gap through the mountains was accomplished in record-breaking time, and when I reached the Piedmont section of North Carolina, the sun began to rise. I had no idea what I was about to face. I stopped along the way and called Eva to get more results from her trip.

I drove straight to the hospital to visit Mom. I would swing by the house later to check on Pappy. When I saw Mom, she was haggard and very gaunt. She had trouble breathing and had to sleep in a propped-up position because her lungs were constantly filling with fluid, and they would have to drain that fluid every so often. This was turning into a no-win scenario, and we didn't know how much longer she would be with us.

When I visited Pappy was agitated and was ranting and raving. He didn't even want to watch baseball on TV. He talked about doctors and hospitals, and he wanted Mom to come home. He said, "Mae needs to come home and if need be, to die at the house."

Deep down inside, I could tell that he was really worried about losing his wife. There was no need to argue or disagree with him. I just sat there and listened and waited for the tempest to pass.

When he settled down somewhat, I introduced him to *The Benny Hill Show*, and Pap thought Benny Hill was very funny and really enjoyed his exploits. I would stay with Pappy throughout the day and would sit up with Mom at night in the hospital.

Usually, Mom would just talk about things and reminisce, but one night she caught me off guard. She looked at me with hurt in her eyes and asked, "Harold, do you think that I should have left your daddy?"

This floored me because there were many times my sister and I felt she should have left Pappy. This was one of the most difficult questions I was ever asked in my entire life. I paused, I knew part of the reason she stayed was my sister and me. I looked at her and answered, "Mom, you did what you thought was right."

Eva called and asked if I could locate the family's important paperwork, such as wills and last rites, etc. So that particular night, I got up enough nerve to ask Mom where this information was located. I was very delicate when I asked Mom this question. Mom didn't take it the wrong way and responded like a trooper.

She told me the important stuff was located on the right side of the second drawer in the chest of drawers in the living room. Hell, even Pappy didn't know where the stuff was. This is why we had to ask Mom. Isn't it amazing that the most important documents of their lives only took up one third of the space in one of those drawers?

During my visit, many visitors came to see Mom; her friends, the people from her church, but the most memorable visitors were her siblings and Grandma Goodman from China Grove. I remember Grandma riding in the elevator, she had this faraway sad look in her eyes. I asked her how she was doing, and she said, "Harold, it is very hard to watch my children die. I wish the Lord would just take me on outa here."

Carl and Becky Blackwelder, who used to live next door, came to visit Mom as well. Carl stated that "Sergeant Shreeve, one of my high school junior ROTC instructors, was also in the hospital, and they are not expecting him to live much longer."

It was as if my entire world that I used to know was coming unraveled all at the same time. I told Carl that I would see Sergeant Shreeve before I returned to Fort Campbell.

When it came time to leave, Pappy came over to the hospital, and I remember Mom sitting on the edge of her bed. She said, "Harold, I am very proud of what you have done."

I told her that I was very proud of her too, but the unspoken connection that was made was that I knew and she knew this was the last time we would see each other alive ever again.

I took the elevator down and paid a last visit to Sergeant Shreeve. He was in a bad way; we had a good talk. We reminisced about a time that was long gone and past but very memorable.

From this, I learned how to say goodbye to someone who meant something to me in my life.

The term *closure* is a way to explain some type of completeness in one's life; however, I have to say there is no such thing for me. Yes, a fond farewell, but the person I am saying goodbye to will always remain as alive, even after they have passed, as the first day I remembered meeting them.

As I walked down the steps of the Cabarrus Memorial Hospital, it felt like the world was caving in on me, and I was not emotionally ready to take the trip back to Fort Campbell in this state of mind. Mr. Pierce, a high school baseball coach and a very prominent mentor in my life, had an office nearby. So I had to visit him before I left. I stopped in, we talked, and he listened to my plight. Somehow I feel that without that visit, I would not have been able to make the trip back home safely.

The return trip was uneventful, except this time the thick fog was located on the Tennessee side of the mountains. The fog was so thick, I could barely recognize that I was passing through Knoxville. I could barely make out the lights that hung over Interstate 40. Time almost seemed to be askew because my mind was constantly drifting back and forth, and what was happening in real time didn't seem to matter.

I eventually made it back to the house in Woodlawn, and after I dragged my tired body back inside, I went into my bedroom and noticed there was a dead bluebird lying on the inside of the windowsill. Evidently, the bluebird's mate found a way inside the house but could not find its way out. That would explain why its mate was trying to get in before I left. The final message that was sent came through loud and clear.

In the midst of this misery, there was a silver lining in this dark cloud. While Mom was in the hospital, Pappy joined the church. While growing up, I never saw Pappy attend church with us. He would drop us off and pick us up at the Westford Methodist Church. Mom prayed for years that her husband would find salvation, and believe it or not, her prayers were finally answered.

It was a joyous but tearful moment when Pappy, this rough and rowdy individual, asked for spiritual help. Brother Ted walked

Pappy down the aisle, and there, at the altar, Ted, Preacher Rodney Quesenberry, and Pappy were crying like babies when Pappy knelt before the altar to receive Jesus, which proves that all things are possible through God.

It was back to the army grind for me. One day, while our unit was on a field exercise at Fort Polk, Louisiana. First Lieutenant Courtney Wright came up to my cot and said, "I am sorry to have to tell you this, but your Mom passed away last night. We are going to get you out of the field and back home as soon as possible."

The first sergeant said, "Don't worry, we will gather up your gear, and we will get you on the next helicopter back to Fort Campbell."

I thanked the top sergeant, proceeded to the tactical operations center (TOC) and called Eva. I asked her to notify the Red Cross so they could expedite my emergency leave.

Then I called my wife Sarah and told her the news. Sarah was a captain in the Army Nurse Corps, who worked as a labor and delivery nurse at the time. I cannot remember the helicopter trip that whisked me back to Fort Campbell.

Sarah and I made the trip. She was to wear her dress greens, and I would wear my dress blues for the ceremony. We stayed at the Quality Inn in Downtown Concord. Eva and I wanted to sing Mom's favorite hymn, "Amazing Grace," together at the ceremony, a capella. So we practiced our rendition the night before.

I could not sleep well that night, so I got up early in the morning to practice my portion of the song. Eva was to sing the first verse, I would sing the second, then we would sing the last verse together. This was very difficult because of the intense emotions we had; we decided to write the lyrics on index cards and hold our cards in front of our faces so we would not see anyone in the audience because if someone in the audience should start to cry, we would start crying and not be able to finish.

I stepped out of the door of the Quality Inn with my index card, and I was overwhelmed with emotions because this motel was right across the street from the Cabarrus Memorial Hospital, where I was born.

Just to my left was a dogwood tree in bloom. This reminded me of the story I was told while growing up. The dogwood bloom represented Christ's crucifixion, the bloom displayed the blood on his head, hands, and feet. This symbol took me to even lower depths of despair. I tried to regain my composure, sat down on a rock, and started singing the first verse, then broke down crying.

I stood up, walked around a bit, and gave another try, only to break down a few verses later. I said to myself, "I am not going to be able to do this."

Just then, I heard a noise behind me, I had not paid much attention to the row of parked cars behind the rock where I was sitting.

There was a guy sleeping in the back seat of one of those cars. Maybe he had a rough night before, but his window was down, and my singing woke him up. I told him I was sorry, and then he looked at me with his sleepy eyes and said, "No, go ahead, it's all right, man, you sound good."

This enabled me to overcome my grief, and I sang my portion of the hymn in front of him with ease.

There were two preachers who spoke at Mom's funeral. Rev. Rick Wilson from the Calvary Foursquare Church, located just across the street from our house, and Preacher Rodney Quesenberry, from Broadus Baptist Church. Eva and I sang our tribute without any trouble. Rodney spoke from Proverbs, then eventually, the ceremony ended, and we proceeded to the burial site.

The place where Mom was laid to rest was at the cemetery behind our house, right beside the small grave marker of my sister that I discovered so many years ago. My friend Terry Gledhill volunteered to take the place as a pall bearer for Uncle Lee Roy, who was not physically capable to carry the coffin.

I could only reminisce about Mom and think about how much the graveyard had expanded since those boyhood days of long ago. They made a cassette tape of the funeral, and I listened to it over and over until it eventually wore out. Yes, Mom was gone.

Chapter 32

A Downhill Slide

After losing Mom, everyone returned to their contemporary endeavors, but her passing marked a rapid decline with Pappy. Mom's friends and fellow church members used to cook for him and deliver meals to the house as an act of kindness. Pappy was thankful and accepted the food graciously, however, he was not used to being pampered in this way.

I remember when Mom was in the hospital, a lady brought Pappy a dish to eat. She stopped by later and asked, "Shad, did you like that casserole plate I fixed for you?"

And he said, "It was good, but them taters were kinda hard." He was use to Mom's cooking.

Pap's lifestyle of drinking, smoking, and breathing cotton dust in the mill had taken a physical toll. Although he had given up strong drink years before, the other faults paved the way for his demise. These facts added to the loss of his lifelong mate was probably the final straw. It was only a matter of time for the grim reaper to appear. The doctor's said he had chronic obstructive pulmonary disease (COPD), and it was a struggle for him to breathe.

He had lived a hard and cruel life; grew up in a family that did not know how to show love; survived the Spanish flu pandemic; lived through the Great Depression; served during WW2, the greatest conflict on earth; saw the rise and fall of the cotton mills; and played baseball with some of the greatest ballplayers there ever were.

He saw America grow, from initially being transported by mule or horse and buggy to the landing on the moon. He lived through fourteen different presidents, from Woodrow Wilson to William Jefferson Clinton, some of which served multiple terms in office. Time was approaching for him to be part of God's lineup.

I have often wondered, by listening to some of those front-porch conversations, that the world in which those of that generation knew had changed so much, they could not recognize it anymore and no longer wanted to be a part of it.

During one of Pappy's last visits to Broadus Church, Preacher Quesenberry asked Pap if he had asked the Lord to forgive him for everything he had done in his life. Pap answered, "No, not everything."

Then Rodney stated, "Well, don't you think you should because you do not have much time left, Shad?"

Pappy dropped to his knees and proclaimed in a loud voice, "Dear Lord, I want you to forgive me for everything I have ever done wrong."

Ted and Rodney had their hands on his shoulders during this last confession, and they helped him to his feet.

Ted told me that Pappy had a bad session at the house just before the final days, so he rushed up to check on Pappy. He told me that Pappy was suffering in a bad way, crawling around on the floor, and did not want to go to the hospital. Ted took him anyway.

While all this was happening, I was far away, on the other side of the world, stationed at Camp Stanley, Korea. Just like before, with Mom's passing, I received a call from Eva, stating that Pappy had died. She was the executor of the will, and she notified the Red Cross so I could come home on emergency leave.

Once again, I notified my wife, who was stationed at Fort Hood at the time. She was to meet me in San Antonio, Texas. From there, we would drive to North Carolina. Things went wrong, and I missed an important change-over flight, and by the time I arrived in San Antonio, it was too late for us to make it to the funeral. We spent that time together before I caught an international flight back to Korea.

Pap passed away on July 15, 1996, just thirteen months to the day after Mom had died. Once again, Preacher Rodney stepped up to the plate and delivered a heartfelt sermon at Pappy's funeral. Just like Red McClamrock's funeral, many came, and for the first time, they learned Pappy's real name, James Manuel Whittington Sr. They only knew him as Shad Rack' his baseball nickname. Pappy was laid to rest beside Mom and Gerldine, at West Concord Cemetery, previously called Union Cemetery.

These were some of the thoughts I had when I was on that return flight to Korea. Pappy was buried at the same place where I remember, as a toddler, watching Vernon Ford and Pappy play peggy behind our house. This was many years before Jeb Kennedy cut the midget car dirt racetrack.

Pappy had given up umpiring and had retired from the mill several years before his death, and I reminisced about the last time I saw him. Near the end, Pappy and many others of his generation were starting to show their age. Those men were stooped and walked with a slight bow, which reminded me of a meaningful poem written by Hank Williams Sr. and was narrated so beautifully by another famous Country and Western singer and songwriter that proceeded as follows:

> *You'll meet many like me upon life's busy street, with shoulders stooped and heads bowed down and eyes that stare in defeat. Or souls that live within the past. where sorrow plays all parts, where a living death is all that's left for men with broken hearts.*
>
> *You have no right to be the judge, to criticize and condemn. just think, for the grace of God, it would be you instead of him. One careless step, a thoughtless deed, and then the misery starts, and for those who weep, death comes cheap, these men with broken hearts. Oh so humble you should be when they come passing by, for it's written that*

> *the greatest men never get too big to cry. Some lose faith in love and life when sorrow shoots her darts, and with hope all gone, they walk alone, these men with broken heart. You've never walked in that man's shoes, or seen things through his eyes, or stood and watched with helpless hands while the heart inside you dies. Some were paupers, some were kings, some were masters of the arts, but in their shame, they're all the same, these men with broken hearts. Life sometimes can be so cruel that the heart will pray for death. God why must these living dead know pain with every breath? So help your brother along the road, no matter where you start. For the God that made you made them too,* these men with broken hearts.

This poem not only reflected the thoughts that I had for Pappy but also all the men of his generation. Why, even the man who recited those words so beautifully, James Travis Reeves, before he became known as Mr. Velvet, was a baseball player from East Texas who pitched for a Saint Louis Cardinal farm team.

After I returned to Camp Stanley, I found out about a situation that happened during Pappy's funeral. A young man by the name of Ansley Burkhalter placed a baseball in Pappy's hand inside the casket. Some who were present thought that was sacrilegious and highly inappropriate; however, I realized that they didn't have a damn clue.

There was a back story to this action that started well before the funeral. Ansley is the son of one of Eva's friends, and he would come up to the house, and of course, Pappy would start talking to him about baseball. These talks sparked Ansely's interest, and he started playing baseball and became a pretty good pitcher. He did this at our beloved Hartsell School.

He pitched so well one day his team won the championship game. The coach gave Ansley that game ball with all the signatures of his team members. This was the baseball he placed in Pappy's hand. Eva, the executor of Pap's will, made the final decision to leave the ball in Pappy's hand.

This is what I have to say about that: Giving our father that game ball was the baseball equivalent to receiving the Medal of

Honor in the military. Of all the accolades Pappy ever received, this was the highest award he could ever be given, and it was presented by a boy who knew its meaning above all others. Ansley was the last person on earth Pappy had mentored from a list that spanned a lifetime.

Years later, I visited my family's grave. I walked through the cemetery and read many different names on the tombstones where they were laid to rest. During which, I found Marvin Mauney's grave. Then I glanced over to where my parents were buried and realized that the distance between those graves were about the same distance between their mill houses when they grew up together on the Franklin Mill Hill.

They started in the same place, went around the world, and ended up almost in the same vicinity. That was amazing, but their trek here on earth is just the beginning of another glorious adventure.

Epilogue

This story ends exactly where it started. I found myself back at Howard's house in Richfield, North Carolina. Howard and I had finished browsing through those baseball pictures, and it was time for me to drive back to Louisiana on that cold February day in 2010.

During the trip, I stopped and got a motel room just before Atlanta, Georgia. After a good rest, I woke up and went to breakfast. While enjoying that good Southern breakfast, I saw a high school baseball team come in. High school teams start early in the season, and I noticed the players as they attacked the buffet but did not envy the conditions they had to practice in. I watched them as they shoveled the food on to their plates, which determined if they were right-handed or left-handed players. I also tried to guess what position they might play based on their body types and stature.

They sat all around me, and by listening to their conversations about their practice, I had guessed their positions better than I realized; however, I remained silent. At that moment, I wondered which one of those athletes would be the next Vernon Ford, Willard Mauney, or Shad Whittington and who would be the scribe who would write their story.

About the Author

William Harold Whittington: Born January 15, 1954, in Cabarrus County, Concord, North Carolina. Raised as a second-generation baseball player. Played Little League, Babe Ruth, high school, and American Legion Baseball while growing up in North Carolina. Served in two branches of the military: first, a four-year tour with the USAF, followed by an eleven-month break, then joined the United States Army until retiring from the army in August 2000 at Fort Hood, Texas, totaling twenty-seven years of active military service, retiring at the rank of a chief warrant officer 4.

While in the USAF, played fast- and slow-pitch softball, which ranged from unit level, base level, and tournament level play in Upper State New York and New Hampshire. Played fast-pitch in Korat, Thailand. Participated in baseball, fast- and slow-pitch softball tournaments while stationed at Nellis AFB near Las Vegas, Nevada. During my air force stretch, worked as an integrated avionics system specialist on the FB-11I and F-111A models.

Joined the army around the summer of 1977, initially as an airborne infantryman then became an electrician on Uh-1H, Oh-58, and Cobra helicopters. Was accepted to helicopter flight school at Fort Rucker, Alabama, in 1978. After flight school, was assigned to Fort Ord, California, with the 2/10 Air Cavalry Squadron. Was stationed at Fort Ord for four and a half years; during which, I played the most extensive levels of fast-pitch softball throughout California to include a tournament in Lake Tahoe, Nevada.

Numerous army tours followed, which gave me the opportunity to play fast- and slow-pitch tournaments throughout Germany, Holland, Korea, and Okinawa. Served as a unit trainer in instrument, tactics, and a UH-1 instructor pilot with night-vision goggles. During the tour in Germany, achieved a Bachelor of Science in Professional Aeronautics with Embry Riddle University 1986.

Transitioned to a Black Hawk UH-60, and after my first assignment at Fort Hood, Texas, attended the Black Hawk test pilot course at Fort Eustis, Virginia, in 1994. After leaving the service, continued to fly helicopters in the Gulf of Mexico for Air Logistics and Bristow Helicopter companies twenty more years. During this time, I eventually ended my ball-playing days by 2013, which spanned forty-nine years.

About the People

Ford, Billy J. Born on the Franklin Mill Hill, December 03,1927, in a mill house on Railroad Avenue.

Without Mr. Bill Ford, this story about my father would have never gotten off the ground. The reason Mr. Ford knew so much was he delivered newspapers as a boy and knew everyone's name and address on the Franklin Mill Hill. He reconstructed the entire Franklin Mill community for me during our five-year-long telephonic interviews. Mr. Ford was the only living member left who knew where the Franklin Mill ballpark was located and how it was constructed.

I was amazed at this man's ability for recall. He was such a treasure trove of information about ball fields and players who had long since vanished by the time I came along. He remained active and played golf with Richard Lefler and Coach Lapish, but then one day, during that period of interviews, I heard he had a stroke, and his memory had faded drastically. There were moments of silence for a while, but he made a comeback.

During our next phone conversation, he told me something that wrenched my heart into several pieces. He said, "Harold, because of my loss of memory, a lot of people were gone out of my life. So I took out my pictures, and newspaper clippings and wrote their names down over and over. Suddenly, they came back into my life."

What a champion. I will let you know tears rolled down my cheeks when I wrote this passage.

There are many more accolades awarded to this man than the notes he forwarded to me. The new Concord High School named their baseball field after him. He was a devout Christian man. I only got to meet him once, but meeting him once was better than knowing a lot of others for a lifetime. Another coincidence is that, if I am not mistaken, we were the only two baseball players from Cabarrus County who played on Soldiers Field in Nuremberg, Germany. He played there in 1952, and I played on that field in 1986.

Unfortunately, Mr. Ford passed away before I could finish this book. During that one-time visit, whenever he would talk about his wife Mildred, who passed away on September 19, 2009. I could see tears well up in his eyes, and you could hear the sadness in his voice. But he was laid to rest beside the love of his life on January 19, 2017, at Mount Olivet Methodist Church. I am sure they are together in heaven.

Coach Ford's Accomplishments

Was a member of Westford Methodist Church and a member of Scout Troop 14.

Attended Hartsell School, played baseball, football, and basketball; and was the president of the senior class of 1947. The year 1947 was the first year that schools in Cabarrus County added the twelfth grade.

After high school, signed a contract with a Cincinnati organization and reported to Muncie, Indiana, in June 1947.

In 1948, returned to Muncie and played all summer and had a good season by hitting 313 as a lead-off hitter and had over five hundred at bats.

In 1949, Ogden, Utah, batted 381 with 130 RBIs. The team finished in sixth place.

In 1950, spring training in Alexandria, Louisiana, then sent to Columbia, South Carolina, played third base, and batted 287.

Mr. Ford told me, "Harold, I married the love of my life on December 23, 1950 at Mount Olivet Methodist Church."

Drafted into the army, was sent to Camp Picket, Virginia, for basic training and spent the summer of '51 playing baseball all over the state of Virginia.

Was MVP in the Virginia State Playoff. As the winner, we went to Kansas to play in the National Playoffs and finished in fifth place. Then back to Camp Pickett, then transferred to Germany for ten months. During my stay in Germany, I had a beautiful daughter in October, and I did not get to see her until September 1952.

In 1953, back to Columbia, we finished in second place that year. I played against Henry Aaron. We beat them in a seven-game playoff, and I hit over three hundred in that series. This is also the time I played with Frank Robinson.

Was sent to Hi-Toms, High Point, Thomasville, North Carolina, in the middle of '55. Spent the rest of my time there, two years with a Red Organization and the last two with the Phillies. During which time, I played with Curt Flood, Dallas Green, and Chris Short, two pitchers who also made it to the big leagues with the Phillies. During this time in winter, I was the athletic director at the Concord Recreational Center while going to college at Catawba.

In 1958, finished college, taught two courses in Mooresville, North Carolina, and coached three sports in junior high.

In 1959, coached senior high football, girls' basketball, and baseball.

In 1960, got a job at Concord High School, coaching football and girls' basketball. Coached American Legion Baseball at Kannapolis, won the league, but lost out to Linc-Cherryville in the playoffs.

In 1961, we won the NC State Championship by beating Hamlet four games to one, then went to Sumpter, South Carolina, and only won one game in the sectional playoffs, but lost two games, 9 to 8.

Nunley, Tom: Born, July 6, 1960, in Alameda, California. Achieved a BA in English Literature at USC. Joined the army in 1978 and retired in 1998. From 1998 through 2020, he worked for Airlog/Bristow Helicopter companies. He was a top-notch mechanic and held various other positions. He currently resides in Dover, Tennessee, with his wife Susan.

Tom has been my editor and critical-writing adviser since the beginning. He gave me the motivation to write when I wanted to quit. We served in the same unit at Fort Hood, Texas, although we did not know each other at the time.

Fortunately, I got to know Tom when we were at New Iberia, Louisiana, while testing helicopters coming out of the hangar after maintenance. He listened to my stories and urged me to put those stories to print. Tom is a consummate professional in many endeavors.

Capra, Frank: My favorite Hollywood director whose movies will always stand out over time. I got the idea for this story from his *Why We Fight Series* he made during WW2, especially the episode "When War Comes to America."

Ford, Vernon Harold: One of the main characters in the book. He was a very important member who came from the Franklin Mill Hill community as well as my father's closest friend. I felt proud of the three home runs I hit out of Hartsell Field in 1976. One of my home runs hit the top of the Hartsell Gym. However, after a historical review of all those home runs hit out of Hartsell Field, my home runs were not so great. Richard Lefler hit one against the gym when he was in high school. Bernie Edwards hit a home run that went through the top of the old poplar tree on the other side of the gym. Hartsell Field was later named Edwards Field in Bernie's honor.

Pappy hit one over the right field fence, which landed on the other side of Swink Street. Vernon Ford hit a home run that landed on top of Hartsell School, you would have to have seen that event to believe it. Vernon Ford was my father's closest friend and the Pied Piper of the community. Children flocked to him as if he was Santa Claus.

Furr, Harold: Another fine man who played with my father in the Yadkin Valley League as well as several seasons with the Roberta Mill team. I was named after him.

Hooks, James Howard Jr.: A classmate and lifelong friend who attended Hartsell and Central Cabarrus schools with me. We were born only seven days apart. He is the son of Howard Hooks Sr., featured in the story, a renowned knuckleball pitcher who played baseball with Pap. We called Howard Sr. Big Howard and his son, my classmate, Little Howard.

When Howard Jr. and I reviewed those baseball albums, it gave me the initial idea to write this book. Little Howard also told stories about his father when he pitched for Albermarle and his father's exploits during the war. Howard Jr. currently resides in Norwood, North Carolina, with his wife Xiomana and their children Alex and Suzanna.

Lapish, Richard: One of father's fellow baseball players. He was my seventh-grade math and science teacher and my Babe Ruth baseball coach for three seasons at Hartsell School. Mr. Lapish was also our driver's education instructor. He taught Billy Edwards, Howard Hooks, and me to drive at Hartsell School.

Mr. Lapish provided the entire lineup for the Concord Patriots for this story. He played softball with my brother Ted for Southside Amaco and Holding Brother's Texaco. I remember riding my bicycle over to visit him and spending time with his amazing Siamese cat Ramesses.

Lefler, Richard: A Hartsell School graduate who shared personal stories during telephonic interviews. He grew up on Short Street and gave me a pitching lesson one day in his front yard. He graduated from Hartsell in 1964 and was the first hitter to hit a home run off the Hartsell School Gym. He was the last great pitcher who came off the Franklin Mill Hill, and the last person who grew up on the hill who made it to the minors.

Parnell, Bryant Jr.: The Parnells were a baseball-playing family from the local area that covered three generations or more. Bryant told me how his family members were related and some of the colorful stories about Fred and Jack Parnell when they played with Pappy.

Stan Parnell, Bryant's younger brother, was my baseball contemporary. We played against each other throughout our Babe Ruth and high school days, and we were on the same American Legion Baseball Team.

When I was thirty years old, I had the privilege to play softball with Bryant and Stan whenever my military schedule would allow. The highlight of that season was when our team won the three-day softball tournament, Sanford, North Carolina, in 1984. Bryant was our pitcher.

Pierce, Jerry: My freshman and sophomore high school baseball coach and outstanding baseball mentor was the first to cover defensive-play situations and various facets of the game many of us did not realize. He taught us how to function as a team and not just a bunch of individuals gathered on a field.

He taught things foreign to us but very basic to him. For example, while I was playing first base, he taught me to keep my foot off the bag until I knew the throw had the runner beat, then tag and immediately get my foot off the bag so I could not be spiked by the runner. To extend my body toward the throw to cut down the time the throw was in the air. If the throw was wide toward the plate, to step on the bag with my right foot and vice versa, if the throw was on the outside of the base.

Most importantly, if the throw was too wide, to leave the bag and go catch the bad throw to hold the other runners in place. I cannot recall how many times those instructions saved me over the course of my years of ball playing.

He was a catcher, and it must be known that a catcher can see everything that is happening on the field, and he knew pitchers. This made him a winning coach. He knew all the other positions in the field as well.

He took the time to catch me in practice for two seasons. He worked on pitch location, selection, and how I should change speeds. After he finished catching, he would get his regular catchers, Reggie McClamrock or Kenny Beck, behind the plate. He taught them how to set up behind the plate to give the pitcher a better target and how to frame a pitch for the umpire. He taught us the battery had to be firmly connected.

Quesenberry, Rodney: Attended Central Cabarrus High School and graduated in 1976. He played football, basketball, and really excelled in track. He participated in the 100-, 220-, and 440-yard dashes and the 880 relay. He was the third-fastest runner in the entire county. However, he had to overcome a physical hardship at a young age.

While he was at Harrisburgh, one of Central's feeder schools, he had a run in with a lawn mower in 1970. The lawn mower cut off half his big toe and half of the one next to the big toe on his right foot. So he had to compensate and learn how to rebalance. Something I had to learn to do much later in life.

Rodney's mental and spiritual changes came after he had twin daughters and the fear of losing them at a young age. The doctors said, "If his twins made it to seven months in the pregnancy, they would be fine."

Rodney confessed that the life he was living at the time was pretty awful. He was smoking, drinking lots of alcohol, using dope, cussing, and being obsessed with women. He became convinced he could not be a good dad living that kind of life. The process changed after he started playing the guitar and writing songs about the Lord.

He learned to give his heart to the real authority by teaching Sunday school and became the youngest deacon ever at Southside Baptist Church. He was asked by one particular preacher to speak one night after they sang, and Rodney told the preacher that he did not speak, and the minister replied, "Yes, you can."

The rest is history, a continuation of that calling.

Rodney finally committed to preaching full time at Camp Wesley in Kanapolis under the guidance of Dr. J. Harold Loman, Rodney's spiritual mentor, holiness preacher, and friend. Rodney's mom called him her little preacher boy.

The following are two examples of his educational efforts: the first without God and the latter after the Lord put him on the right path. The first time they recruited him to attend Catawba College and play football for a year, they wanted him to play without a scholarship that first year. Well he just partied all year and later transferred to UNCC. He flunked out at UNCC the second year and got married. He was twenty-eight years old and became the father of twins, and then God stepped into his life.

This is what happened after God took over. Rodney went back to school at UNCC for the remainder of his degree. He reactivated his Veterans Scholarship there and graduated in two years, which included summer sessions. Rodney received a degree majoring in religious studies with a minor in criminal justice and social work. He made the dean's list every time afterward. So I will ask the readers, which path would you chose, if offered a choice?

After UNCC, he was provided a par-time job at a bank that offered perfect hours so he could finish school and still support his family. He received his master's and doctoral degrees from Bethany Seminary in Dothan, Alabama, through the extension and online program, and went there for the graduation exercises.

Rodney came to Broadus in May 1989. He has been preaching there for thirty-three years, with thirty-eight years total of pastoring to date. When he came to Broadus was where he really came to know my mom, sister Eva, brother Ted, Pappy, and eventually me.

Rodney's father also served in WW2. So proper credit must be given to Robert Lee Quesenberry Sr., who came from the coal mines of Southern West Virginia. He served as a first sergeant of the first division, combat engineers, part of the Big Red One. If you study that division's progress during WW2, you will never be able to render the proper words, nor shower enough accolades to commend what those men accomplished.

Rodney's mom, Peg Gray Quesenberry, whom I have never met, indirectly gave me the incentive to start writing my short stories. I read a book called *Lunch in a Lard Bucket*, and she was the author of one of the stories in that book. *Lunch in a Lard Bucket* is a compilation of short stories written by regular people, which included down-to-earth episodes of life in Cabarrus County. Maybe someday, if I make the grade, I will get to meet her and shake her hand.

While I was away in the military, my sister Eva called me and told me that Ted and Carolyn had joined the church at Broadus. I told Eva, "My God, Bonnie and Clyde joined the church."

I never thought that would happen, but no one should ever try to put limits on our Maker.

Rodney has proofread everything I have written. Because I wanted my stories to have the proper spiritual oversight. I spent many hours on the phone with Rodney while writing this book, asking questions about my father's and brother Ted's last moments of their lives. Rodney preached at Mom's, Pappy's, and brother Ted's funerals.

Before Ted passed away, I told Rodney I promised Ted if anything ever happened to him, that I wished to speak at his funeral. Rodney granted me that wish. This was the greatest favor I have ever received. How many preachers do you know would give up their pulpits and allow a person not even a member of their church the opportunity to speak directly to their congregation?

Mauney, Willard Sr.: Another one of Pap's friends who grew up on the Franklin Mill Hill, who played several years in the Minor Leagues, which included many seasons with the Concord Weavers and one season with the Greenville Greenies.

Willard also joined the navy and served in WW2. His son Willard Jr. stated his father was assigned to the USS *Hornet* but somehow missed the launch date or was reassigned to another vessel. On October 27, 1942, the *Hornet* was sunk, and 140 sailors lost their lives. Willard could have been one of those 140.

Willard played for Roberta after his Minor League jaunt and umpired baseball and softball games with my father for many years on Gibson, Randolph, Webb, Macalister, Hartsell, and Central Cabarrus fields. Willard lived in Roberta until his passing.

The following players were from the Mauney family: Luke, Willard, Richard, Marvin, and Harold. What a lineup.

> **Luke:** Willard's elder brother, played baseball and fast-pitch softball with Pappy, and is shown in the Franklin Mill fast-pitch team picture, along with Willard.
>
> **Richard:** Willard's younger brother, who was very close to Pappy, the only pitcher from Hartsell

School who made it to the Major Leagues. He pitched for the Philadelphia Phillies.

Marvin: Richard's younger brother, played several years in the Minor Leagues with the Morganton Aggies in the Western Carolina and in the North Carolina state leagues. Marvin served in WW2 under General Patton.

Harold: The youngest of the Mauney boys, was my first season Little League coach for Hartsell School. I played my first organized game at Randolph Field under his coaching. It was obvious that my area was deeply intertwined with baseball.

McClamrock, Rick: A high school classmate of mine, Red McClamrock's youngest son. He gave me the full story of how his father met his fate during that horrific car wreck that dreadful night. Twins Kenny and Reggie are Rick's elder brothers. I played against the McClamrock brothers on Randolph Field and spent three seasons with them at Central Cabarrus High School.

I really got to know Rick and his family after brother Ted moved in next door to the McClamrocks on Branch Drive. Rick currently resides in Concord, North Carolina, and owns Pots of Luck Florist Shop.

Utley, Hank: The coauthor of *The Independent Carolina Baseball League*, a story about Concord's first attempt at a professional baseball team. Hank worked with the Boys Club of America and provided information about Minor League players, and one colorful story I included in this book about his baseball adventure was while playing at Roberta. He also told another story that can only be repeated, in private, when Tommy Lasorda left the Concord Weavers to join the army in 1945.

Hank would send me pictures of ball teams and ask me if I could name any of the players. Well, he sent one that was over the top. It featured a team picture of a group of ballplayers dressed in uniforms that teams wore in the gay '90s or sometime around the turn of the century. The manager of the team had a curved waxed mustache like Snidely Whiplash from the *Dudley Do-Right* cartoons. It was impossible for me to name any of the players, but I did recognize the field where the picture was taken. The photo was taken at Randolph Field, already the name of the field when I played there; originally, it was known as Locke Field, when the photo in question was taken. Currently, there is an apartment complex called Locke Mill Plaza, but the ball field was located on the other side of Peach Street, behind the old Coca-Cola plant, no longer exists.

Hank wanted me to write a book about the Carolina Textile Baseball League, but I told him that was beyond my scope and reminded him I was not James Michener. I wanted to limit the story within a smaller focus about ballplayers who originated from Franklin, Hartsell, and Brown-Norcott mills.

Unfortunately, I never got to meet Hank. I only knew him through our phone conversations while writing Pappy's story. My greatest regret was that Hank passed away before I got to finish this book. I would have liked that he had been able to review and critique my story. I hope he would have approved.

Whittington, Eva: My younger sister, born October 16, 1960, who later married Andrew Self, and currently resides in Hopkinsville, Kentucky. She provided me with a myriad of pictures and our parents' love letters hidden away in the chest of drawers. She was responsible for a book called *Mae Bell's Daughter,* which goes into greater depth about what I covered in chapter 30.

Whittington, James Manuel Sr.: My father, the main character of the story, also known as Shad Rack. I am thankful I listened to his stories while growing up and could recall most of those descriptions. He was a master raconteur who possessed abilities that would stagger one's mind. Despite his shortcomings, I was honored to have a dad like him. He taught me everything he knew, and I hope someday we will meet again.

Whittington, Mae Bell: Born September 8, 1926, in Rowan County, North Carolina. The first daughter of William Thomas and Ida Goodman. Mae grew up with eight other siblings. Mae was a hard worker; she tended to farm animals, worked the fields, and worked at Plant 1 in Kannapolis with Cannon Mills. She married James Whittington Sr., June 10, 1947, in South Carolina and was a very devoted wife. On January 15, 1954, at Cabarrus Memorial Hospital, she gave birth to me. She was a devout Christian throughout her life, our families only conduit to God. She taught us how to pray, and she introduced us to Jesus Christ.

Whittington, Ted: My elder brother, born in January 1938 on the Franklin Mill Hill. Ted gave me the full story about how he grew up on the hill and the time he and his elder brother JM Jr. spent at Sipes Orphanage Home. Unfortunately, Ted passed away on April 8, 2014, before I finished the book.

Verble, Gene Kermit Sr.: Born June 29, 1928, on the Hartsell Mill Hill. He is the son of Ralph Verble, who played baseball with my father. I played baseball with his son Gene (Skip) Verble Jr. for two seasons at Central Cabarrus High School. Skip was our third baseman.

Gene graduated from Hartsell School in 1947. Gene and Bill Ford were classmates. Gene played professional baseball for seventeen years and was the only other Hartsell student who made it to the Majors. His nickname was Satchel. He played shortstop for the Washington Senators in 1951, and part of the '53 season, Pappy told me, Gene was considered to be the best glove in the South.

Gene spent time playing in the Southern Association, with the Atlanta Crackers and the Chattanooga Lookouts. He managed in the Washington/Minnesota Twins organization from 1957 to 1961 with the Charlotte Hornets and was named Manager of the Year for two seasons of that five-year stint. Gene was another of those players I interviewed over the phone, and here are some of the stories he told me during those calls. Gene talked about when he and Richard Mauney were playing for the Atlanta Crackers. This was years after Richard had pitched for the Philadelphia Phillies. Gene stated, "Richard had just unpacked his suitcase, sat down on the bed, looked up at me, and said, 'I don't know what the hell I am doing here, I need to go back home to Albermarle." Richard repacked his suitcase and left.

Gene told me about the time Pappy shot that bird off the water tower near the store. Ralph Verble was the original owner of the store, called Jackson Park Grill, a gas station and convenience store located in the mouth of the Y intersection of the old Charlotte Highway and Wilshire Drive.

When Gene took over the store, it was called Gene's Short Stop. It was the meeting place for all the ballplayers, where they would sit, sip on a soft drink, and talk baseball. Those meetings were much richer than what could be found on the Internet or what the World Wide Web could offer. I received my information person to person.

I was saddened because I heard that Gene's eyesight was starting to fail, and during our last phone call, Gene said, "Harold, yes, I made the Majors, but there were several ballplayers that came off those mill hills that were better than me, and your daddy was one of them."

Gene passed away at Hospice House of Cabarrus County, November 4, 2017. I am sure he has joined the Valhalla of baseball players. I keep his obituary from the *Independent Tribune* in my wallet and will do so until the ink fades away or until I die.

References

Salmond, John. *Gastonia 1929: The Story of the Loray Mill Strike.* University of North Carolina Press, 1995.

Davis, B. J. "Walking Out: The Great Textile Strike of 1934." *Tar Heel Junior Historian*, Spring 2010.

Davis, Scott. *North Carolina's World War II Experience.* Documentary. Directed by Scott Davis. 2016. Public Broadcast System, 2016. Television.

Sipes Orchard Home History, https://www.sipesorchardhome.org/.

Utley, R. G. (Hank) and Verner, Scot. *The Independent Carolina Baseball League.* McFarland & Company, 1999.

Williams, Hank, Sr. *"Men with Broken Hearts."* 1951.

Printed in the United States
by Baker & Taylor Publisher Services